The State and the S
An International Per

The State and the School
An International Perspective

Edited by

John D. Turner

 Falmer Press

(A member of the Taylor & Francis Group)
London • Washington, D.C.

UK   The Falmer Press, 4 John Street, London WC1N 2ET
USA The Falmer Press, Taylor & Francis Inc., 1900 Frost Road, Suite 101, Bristol, PA 19007

First published in 1996

A catalogue record for this book is available from the British Library

Library of Congress Cataloging-in-Publication Data are available on request

ISBN 0 7507 0477 2 cased
ISBN 0 7507 0478 0 paper

Jacket design by Caroline Archer

Typeset in 11/13 pt Garamond by Graphicraft Typesetters Ltd., Hong Kong.

Printed in Great Britain by Biddles Ltd., Guildford and King's Lynn on paper which has a specified pH value on final paper manufacture of not less than 7.5 and is therefore 'acid-free'.

Contents

Introduction

John D. Turner

'To whom do schools belong' was the question posed by the title of a book by W.O. Lester Smith, a book which was well-known to earlier generations of educationists. In 1942 the question was so novel that it scarcely needed asking. The normal definition seemed a perfectly acceptable one, that the British system of education was 'a national system locally administered'. In my early professional career I derived a great deal of satisfaction from telling students from other countries that in Britain the State employed virtually no teachers, that there was no national curriculum, the head teacher of each school being responsible for the curriculum of that school, that the State's views on methodology were contained in a frequently revised *Handbook of Suggestions for Teachers* and that the 1944 Education Act had been scrupulous in insulating the Minister of Education from the work of the schools. There was a general agreement that education was too important to be left to politicians.

Now the view in Britain is rather that education is too important to be left to teachers. Whereas the curriculum and syllabus were previously the concern of the professionals, the Government now deeply distrusts professionals, not just in education but in every profession. The Secretary of State has assumed massive powers in a series of Education Acts, and there is a National Curriculum which is not just a curriculum but which intrudes into the detail, and often the fine details, of the syllabus. It is the Secretary of State who tells us when 'history' stopped and what books constitute 'literature'. The teachers themselves are subject to constant instruction and criticism, while the progress of students is measured by a series of externally administered tests, which do not command the support of the majority of teachers. The results of the tests are published, for the information of parents, in a series of 'league tables'. The twin concepts of accountability and cost effectiveness are now as common in discussions about education as they are in discussions of industry and commerce.

Nor are these trends restricted to any level of education or to any one country. They are as widespread in the great universities as they are in the primary schools, they are on the agenda not only in Britain and Europe, but in Australia, the United States and indeed virtually every country in the developed and the developing world. The chapters in this book deal with many different cultures and many different countries from several different continents, but the central theme is universal and of great significance: the contributors to the volume, however, hold widely divergent views.

On the one hand are those like Richard Pring, who value the liberal tradition in education. He, and others like him, believe that education is:

> the initiation of a learner by a teacher into the conversation which takes place between the generations of mankind in which the learner is introduced to the voices of poetry and literature, of history and of philosophy, of science and religion. The State's job is to make that conversation possible — not to structure it . . . Teachers play the central part in this practice of education. They are the central players. They mediate the culture — the conversation between the generations. They have the knowledge both of that which needs to be passed on and of the state of receptiveness of the learner. It is a difficult and delicate task — and one that requires both kinds of expertise.

This view is shared by a number of the contributors. They see the intrusion of the State into detailed educational issues not just as foolish, since the Government does not possess the skills and knowledge which would permit it to make good decisions, but also as threatening academic freedom. This is a threat to which Dr Mkandawire points as he considers it in the African context.

He argues that repression of academic freedom 'constitutes only a part of the matrix of the violation of human rights and the web of authoritarian rule'. It is one of the signs by which, he says, incipient or actual tyranny and repression can be recognized; for that reason such repression is to be strenuously resisted.

Some of the other contributors, however, do not see the situation quite so clearly. They draw attention to the rights of the various stakeholders in the education enterprise, the parents and the children, as well as the right of those who pay for the enterprise, to insist on obtaining value for money. Is it not true that the professionals have been allowed to escape public scrutiny for decades, and to work without close scrutiny either of their methods or of the quality of their product?

Partington believes that parents who have a choice of school require the same quality of factual information as they would expect if they were buying a car. He is not prepared to accept 'educational monopoly without adequate monitoring and public information'.

One country which is quite clear about the role of the State in education is Chile, as Beatrice Avalos-Bevan indicates:

> From a past history in which the State was mainly responsible for educational provision and where education was described in the 1925 Constitution as having the 'preferential attention of the State', the new Organic Law for Education (1989) defined the role of the state as largely a subsidiary one, and opened the education system to competitive bids in the market square.

It is fascinating to see the movement towards teacher and school control of the curriculum moving, as in a number of other countries, in a diametrically opposite direction to that in Britain, and it is interesting to note Beatrice Avalos-Bevan's view that in both Britain and Chile the reforms are a response, not to changes in educational theory, but to the political strategy of the party in power. Her study of the interaction of political and theoretical assumptions in the determination of educational policy draws richly on the systems of education in a number of countries, but particularly that of Chile, and her classification of educational issues indicates the similarity of current matters of concern as much as it underlines the variety of solutions which are being applied. It is our task to decide whether to increase our work on those issues which still require definitive research, or whether, since decisions are made predominantly on the basis of political reality, such research is unlikely radically to affect the situation.

The question of public choice in education is examined also by Joe Stetar who concentrates on private higher education in the United States. His study is not relevant only to that context, however. In many developing, as well as richer countries, private institutions are often regarded as an important way of extending educational opportunities with minimal cost to the state. In the CIS and other former communist countries experiments in private education are already taking place. Stetar suggests that the relevant question is not 'Will the need of a nation to infuse new life and vigour into its higher education system cause educational leaders to experiment with privatization?' but rather 'Can such countries, trying to recover from the constrictions of highly centralized planning and control afford not to have a vibrant private sector of higher education?'. But the accompanying question is 'How will quality be assured in such a system of privatized higher education?'.

3

This question, a relatively new one in higher education in Britain but of longer standing in the United States where the difference of achievement among different institutions has long been recognized, is a difficult one to answer at all levels of education.

Many people are now thinking and writing about school quality and school effectiveness, which is another relatively new entry in educational indices. When a topic can give birth to a specialist journal one can assume that it is a respectable subject for research! There is now a thriving literature dealing with the characteristics of the good school. Not everyone, however, would agree that it is easy to recognize a good school when we see one. Indeed Lynn Davies argues that the State could not tolerate a fully effective school system. In good schools:

> more and more children would pass examinations. More and more children and parents would have high expectations of their futures. Demand for the next level of education would increase dramatically. Demand for jobs associated with high achievement at school and beyond would increase similarly . . . *Really* improving school effectiveness in terms of full academic achievement for all would lead swiftly to a situation totally out of control . . . (In England) every time the examination results show a rise in standards, powerful sectors within the Department for Education claim that standards of assessment must be falling and that more means worse . . . The immediate response when the system appears too successful is to instigate immediate 'reforms', sidetracking schools and teachers onto other activities to diminish their efficiency.

The same factors, says Davies, operate in developing countries:

> taking the cynical view, schooling in many developing countries is highly effective for what it is needed for. It provides avenues for the few to gain specialized knowledge while containing the mass in the myth of opportunity and promise . . . It is important not to have too many (high achieving schools), otherwise the shaky pyramid of selection starts to bulge and crack.

It is a frightening diagnosis.

Lynn Davies' chapter is not the only one which considers the role of the State in education in developing countries. Fiona Leach examines the reasons why so many educational projects fail to produce the intended results. She argues that the organizational culture within the projects is incompatible with that of the host institutions in which the projects are housed and that neither of the two obvious courses of action will meet the difficulty. Neither attempting to make the host institution more like the project in its organizational culture nor bringing the culture of the project closer to that of the host institution is likely to be effective. In particular her recognition that 'Third World officials are . . . highly skilled and intelligent executives who manage the system with a great efficiency to meet their own interests' will strike an answering chord in many international consultants. She argues that:

> what may appear to be structural weaknesses and irrational behaviour to the outsider are in fact structural strengths and quite rational behaviour from the inside, where the exercise of personal power, confusion, vagueness, low levels of account-ability and reduced performance targets are advantages to the individual with a personal agenda.

The chapters of this book were, in their original form, papers given at the third Oxford Conference on Education and Development held at New College, Oxford, under the aegis of the *International Journal of Educational Development*. In view of the perennial interest and importance of the issues involved it is unlikely to be the last time that the changing role of the State in educational development will appear on the conference agenda. In the meantime, the chapters contained in this volume will clarify many of the most important issues which must be resolved.

John D. Turner

1   The State and the Teacher in England and Wales

Richard Pring

Liberal Education

Education, formally speaking, is a transaction which takes place between teacher and learner — between one who is in possession of knowledge and skills and one who wants to possess them. It requires no civil authority, only a desire to learn, a desire to impart that learning and facilities to enable the twain to meet.

Education, so conceived, has a life of its own — so long as there are people who want to learn and people who want to teach. And, therefore, teachers see themselves in a long tradition whose heroes and heroines are great teachers, people who inspired, moved the imagination, shed light where there was ignorance. Such people might be seen as stages in the growing understanding which the next generation benefitted from, extended and passed on to others.

The idea of an educational tradition is an important one — the idea of a mode of working and a way of understanding which develop through some sort of internal principles, as in this case the principles of criticism, of enquiry, of questioning, whilst at the same time respecting the foundations upon which that criticism or enquiry or questioning is based. The tradition of 'liberal education' has always asserted the importance of text — key texts which become the touchstones of subsequent development, a common element in different understandings, a source of unity in the diverse solutions offered to a problem. For example, different philosophical viewpoints expounded in our universities will constantly refer back, critically or positively, to the Dialogues of Socrates or the *Nichomachaean Ethics* of Aristotle, to Mill's *Essay on Liberty* or to Hume's *Essay on Human Nature*. Similarly, there is a canon of 'good literature' which helps define such a tradition in English, or key musical creations which determine particular traditions within music.

I am well aware of the problems in saying this — as the sociologists of knowledge have regularly pointed out. But that matters not at all. My point is that central to the public world of education in which we privately participate, there is a continuity of intellectual and aesthetic development, based on criticism and enquiry, and transmitted from one generation to the next through the transaction which takes place between teacher and pupil. Schools and universities are places where that transaction takes place.

In such a view of an educational tradition, the State has a minimal role. It has no *necessary* place. Indeed, it is to be feared, because so easily can it use its power to distort that development, to twist it to its own ends, to end the free spirit of enquiry and criticism because these might subvert the very state itself.

However, although it has no essential role in the transaction itself, it may be necessary to ensure the context in which the transaction between teacher and learner might take place — buildings, teachers, libraries, laboratories, books etc. One can imagine situations where that transaction between teacher and pupil is made impossible, and where an educational tradition is ended. Books are destroyed; libraries closed; publications censored; schools razed to the ground. And, therefore, the State has a role in protecting that tradition. However, it is a facilitating role.

The 1944 Education Act established secondary education for all for the first time in England and Wales. It was thought that everyone had the right to participate in that tradition — according to age, ability and aptitude. And the role of the State was to ensure that such a right might be exercised. The requirement of the State to ensure proper educational provision was interpreted as a minimum involvement. Indeed, when, under the 1944 Education Act, a Central Advisory Council was established with the statutory obligation of the Minister to consult it, the then Permanent Secretary, John Maude, explained to Dr Marjorie Reeves, a member of the Council, the main job of the Councillor:

> to die at the first ditch as soon as politicians try to get their hands on education.

There was nothing controversial in such a view. Government's job was to ensure the framework through which that transaction between teacher and learner might be achieved — not influence the transaction itself.

The political philosophy which determined this limited role of the State reflected a tradition of liberal education, already referred to, which was the inheritance of those who framed the legislation and implemented it. Indeed, these were themselves the products of a tradition of public service rooted in a liberal tradition whose essential task was to facilitate, to make possible, rather than to provide. Schools, therefore, were not (and strictly speaking still are not) *state* schools; they are Church schools or local authority schools, though *maintained* by the State.

There are, of course, various interpretations of that liberal tradition, but the following seem to be common features.

First, it is essentially about (to use Newman's words) the perfection of the intellect. Intellect might be interpreted generously or narrowly, to include knowledge and understanding, or to include as well aesthetic appreciation and moral sensitivity. But, whatever the internal debate, it is about learning which develops the mind by removing ignorance and opening it up to fresh ideas.

Second, that intellect is perfected through introduction to the different forms of knowledge and appreciation through which experience is shaped and understood.

Third, those different forms are defined in terms of key ideas and concepts, specific mental processes and skills, which need to be learnt — and learnt from those who have already mastered them.

Fourth, the authorities within these intellectual traditions, the arbiters of standards, the experts who can direct the learning and say what is right or wrong, are the historians, the scientists, the mathematicians whose ideas and judgment have withstood criticism and have been corroborated through the scrutiny of others. They are accepted as experts amongst their peers — having subjected themselves to critical examination.

Fifth, the purpose of learning — of being initiated into these various modes through which the intellect is perfected — requires no justification beyond the satisfaction that the initiation brings. It is worthwhile in itself. It is so worthwhile that, according to many, the State, although not obviously the beneficiary, is obliged to support it. Universities, for example, since they are too expensive to stand on their own feet, should nonetheless continue to be supported in the pursuit of studies (ancient Egyptian, anthropology, medieval history, Old Norse) which possess no obvious usefulness. It is the prerogative of those *within* the educational tradition to decide what is of most worth — not the state, even though that prerogative must depend on state support.

Sixthly, therefore, the liberal tradition best flourishes in institutions insulated against the noise, business and 'relevance' of the world — a monastic form of life in which the intellect and imagination can reign freely.

In a nutshell, the liberal tradition sees education to be (in the metaphor borrowed from Oakeshott) the initiation of a learner by a teacher into the conversation which takes place between the generations of mankind in which the learner is introduced to the voices of poetry and literature, of history and of philosophy, of science and of religion. The State's job is to make that conversation possible — not to structure it.

The authorities — those who set the standards — are people who have been successfully introduced to these different intellectual and aesthetic traditions. They are to be found certainly in universities, as centres of learning, scholarship and research, but elsewhere as well. And teachers are, more often than not, rooted in such centres through their own education and training and through continued contact.

Teachers, therefore, play the central part in this practice of education. They are the central players. They mediate the culture — the conversation between the generations. They have the knowledge both of that which needs to be passed on and of the state of receptiveness of the learner. It is a difficult and delicate task — and one that requires both kinds of expertise.

Teaching as a Profession

Teachers claim, therefore, to be professionals in the following senses. First, they, like doctors or lawyers, claim an expertise which separates them from lay people, by virtue of which learners come to them for help. That expertise lies in a knowledge of what is to be transacted between teacher and learner; but it lies, too, in being able to translate that knowledge into a mode that is comprehensible and accessible to the learner.

Second, the teacher is a professional through the acquisition of those values which shape the distinctive relations between professional and client — the caring for the integrity of that which is to be learnt, a disdain for those who lie or 'cook the books', an insistence upon standards of elegance and clarity, a contempt for the superficial or trivial explanations, a demand for standards appropriate to the subject matter. The literature teacher is concerned if not passionate about the standards of literacy appreciation and criticism which are internal to the tradition itself. Such professional values are such as to be a bulwark against State interference or State persuasion — the children's educational welfare takes precedence over the State's demands.

Thirdly, by virtue of this expertise and attachment to an independent tradition of enquiry, the teacher, as a professional, would claim some responsibility for its own standards of performance, qualification for entry, disciplinary procedures etc. This is the basis of the teachers' claim in England and Wales for a General Training Council such as obtains in Scotland. But note what this means. It means restriction on State interference, a denial of State authority in defining what are appropriate standards of performance and of behaviour.

Teachers in England and Wales have never achieved the status of professional in any formal sense — there is no equivalent to the General Medical Council for doctors or to the Bar Council for lawyers. But the essentially professional nature of teachers, entailing an independence of State control and interference, has played a significant part in the definition of the relationship between State and teachers.

The minimal role of the State as established in the wake of the 1944 Education Act was reflected in the creation in 1964 of the Schools Council — after the abortive effort of the Minister of Education to create within the Ministry a Curriculum Study Group. That failed, as the 'hidden garden of the curriculum' remained closed to ministers — that was a professional matter. But the Schools Council, arising from its ashes, was a different matter. In overall charge of the teachers themselves, though dependent on state support, it produced research and development which would aid, not be a substitute for, the professional judgment of the teachers. Furthermore, that research and development reached way beyond the teaching of a subject. As Morrell, the Civil Servant who was the main architect of the Schools Council, said in the Joseph Payne Lecture of 1965:

> Jointly we need to define the characteristics of change — relying, whenever possible, on objective data rather than on opinions unsupported by evidence. Jointly, we need to sponsor the research and development work necessary to respond to change. Jointly, we must evaluate the results of such work, using both judgment and measurement techniques . . . Jointly, we need to recognize that freedom and order can no longer be reconciled through implicit acceptance of a broadly ranging and essentially static consensus on educational aims and methods.

In other words, his vision (now sadly lost) was of a forum within which and through which the teachers themselves could identify curriculum and assessment problems, through which they, at the very centre of the conversation between the generations of mankind, could explore the strategies for improved learning; through which they, with their intimate front line knowledge of educational problems, could sponsor the research and development which were needed.

Problems

All that has changed. Morrell's institution, if not his vision, is dead. The Central Advisory Councils have been wound up. The State has entered the 'hidden garden'. There is no General Teaching Council. Departments of Educational Studies are threatened with closure unless they toe the Government's line.

What has happened? And is that tradition of liberal education, so dependent on State support and yet so dependent on freedom from State interference, now threatened? Does the authority of the scholar give way to the power of the State? And must the teacher claiming to be a professional now finally admit to being a technician — carrying out the State's job according to the State's specifications, no longer at the centre of the stage, no longer controlling the transaction that takes place between teacher and learner?

There are four reasons why this relationship between State and teacher has changed — from a relationship between provider and professional to one between architect and artisan of the educational system:

Accountability

The first problem concerns the accountability of those who are professionals. We have seen an unprecedented attack on professionals of every sort, including doctors, lawyers, and social workers, questioning the extent of their authority and the devolved power that goes with it. That questioning has rarely threatened the technical skills and the expert knowledge and understanding (of, for example, medical cure or criminal law) but it has questioned privileged knowledge about aims, purposes or values. The liberal tradition saw those, too, to be within the authoritative expertise of the scholar — of the academic community. The dons of Cambridge would adjudicate the 'Great Tradition' of literature; the dons of Oxford the key philosophical texts. Books in justification were written, but very much to people within the tradition. Little accountability to an outside world was thought necessary.

But that is no longer the case. It was felt that standards, whatever they are, were in decline — that those who professed education were failing in their duty. Either too many learners were failing to come up to these standards or the standards themselves were being redefined in an unacceptable way — the terms, for example, of the student-centred tradition of John Dewey. Indeed the attack on John Dewey from the

Black Paper onwards became quite virulent — the archdemon of the left-wing softies. A systematic attack on the autonomy of those who operated at least within the political freedom and independence of the liberal tradition was mounted and entered into the political arena. In the 1970s and 1980s, the state gradually entered the secret garden of the curriculum, finally defining those standards and enshrining these within a National Curriculum, upon which could be hung 'performance indicators' — assessments by which the achievement of teachers and schools might be measured. Standards, once a matter of mystery to the outside world, became publicly visible.

Cost

The consensus following the 1994 Education Act over the distinctive roles of State and profession — the one providing the resources, the other controlling the shape and the content of the curriculum — was always vulnerable. It depended on those who are in positions of power being convinced of their own limited role — the importance of preserving the independence of scholarship, research and learning. It depended on the State finding no objection to paying the money for something which it refused to affect. But the temptation not to be so restrained must always be there. Once universities become dependent on State money, then they are vulnerable to State interference. It is correct that, if the Secretary of State does not like the Department of Educational Studies at the University of Oxford, he has the power to close it down — not by persuading the Vice Chancellor of the need but by cutting off the money.

The cost of education is £16 billion. It is a very expensive commodity. At a time of recession and at a time of ever increasing demand for education, so the effectiveness (however that is measured) of education becomes greater cost-effectiveness which affects the educational ideal itself. Universities are having to put in place systems of 'quality control' and 'quality assurance', incorporating 'performance indicators' and demonstrating 'value addedness' which change the very nature of that transaction between teacher and learner. The metaphor of a conversation between the generations of mankind — the quality of which is so hard to measure — succumbs to the metaphor of a service given by a provider to a customer. The authority of the educator gives way to the satisfaction of the customer — more easily measured in the overall pursuit of efficiency and effectiveness of a costly service.

Economic Relevance

Many have been the attacks on the economic relevance of education — these partly pointing to the failure of schools to make literate and numerate so many young people, but (more deeply than that) pointing also to the chasm between the liberal tradition and economic utility. The State, investing so much money in education and believing that there should be a connection between that investment and economic performance, feels the right to change the nature of that transaction between teacher and learner so that it serves a different set of purposes. No longer should the ends to be served be defined within the intellectual and aesthetic tradition; rather should they be defined by economic need. No longer are the authorities the recognized scholars within these academic traditions; rather are they the employers or economic analysts who can analyze the skills and knowledge required to do a job competently. Judgment of quality gives way to measurement of performance against pre-defined criteria. Research is not pursued because of problems that arise from within the life of the academic discipline, but is sponsored by bodies (in particular Government departments such as the Ministry of Defence or of Health) who are looking for useful outcomes. Furthermore, the results of such research is increasingly treated as the property of the sponsors rather than as the property of the research community.

Social Control

The fourth reason why the State feels that it cannot remain indifferent to the content and character of education is that education is a matter of changing the consciousness of the learner — introducing the learner to ideas about the quality of life and the goals that are worth pursuing. Particularly is this the case when education is rapidly extended beyond a small elite to a much more representative sample of the population as a whole. The power of ideas cannot be easily dismissed. Therefore, in the National Curriculum, the Secretary of State has arrogated to himself the power to determine the detailed content of the curriculum in each subject. He even decided that history ended in 1962.

The fear is reflected in the research of Stewart Ranson. Senior Civil Servants in the Treasury and the Department of Education declared:

Contrary to popular myth education has been too successful. We can cope with the Toxteths and Brixtons. We do not know whether we can cope with future social unrest. Once again children must learn to know their place.

When the Youth Training Scheme, under the erstwhile Manpower Services Commission, started its programmes for preparing young people more effectively for work, modules of social and economic awareness were terminated. Personal and social education was redesignated personal effectiveness.

The problems of that liberal tradition, therefore, are seen to be: first, the lack of accountability of the educators themselves to an outside world which, rightly or wrongly, questions the efficacy with which the academic community preserves standards of good learning; second, the concern of the 'good housekeeper' wanting to see greater efficiency in State investment; thirdly, the determination to redirect the educational enterprise to economically useful ends — without deliberation about those ends being a necessary part of the educational experience; finally, the fear of the subversive effect of education, ideas in history or literature, in politics or in sociology which might undermine shared social and economic purposes.

Changing Role of the State

The precise way in which the State responds to such matters is still unfolding and, indeed, it is not easy to predict quite the state of affairs that will emerge. The resistance of a liberal tradition is strong — and has its own power and authority. Indeed, there are contradictions within the emerging ideas in terms of which intervention is either justified or restrained.

On the one hand, as we have seen, the State no longer takes the minimalist role adopted after the 1944 Education Act, namely, that of ensuring the resources (buildings and qualified teachers) and a proper legal framework. It is much more interventionist to the extent of detailed control over the curriculum, over the qualification of teachers, even over the continuation of prestigious university departments if they fail to toe the political line. Under the 1988 and 1993 Education Acts the Secretary of State has acquired hundreds of new powers such that there is little that cannot be determined by his/her political wish. The history, English and music attainment targets and programmes of study have all been rewritten at the bidding of Secretaries of State, against the judgment of professionals and academics both on and off the working parties. The Secretary of State has decided what is good literature to read and music to appreciate, as well as when history stops.

This control is exercised through 'quangos' — non-accountable bodies of political appointees. Gone are the advisory councils, and the buffers against central control, namely, the local authorities. These have been so enfeebled as to be practically of no consequence. The politicians have their hands on education and no one has died at the first ditch.

On the other hand, the talk is of 'rolling back the powers of the State', of transferring the running of the schools from bureaucracy to the schools themselves and their communities, and the choices which will be either responsive or indifferent to the choosing public. Choice and freedom are the watchwords. The framework is a market, the regulation of which is carefully controlled centrally, but a market none-theless within which freedom of choice is pursued. To exercise that choice intelligently the public need to have clear statements about the content of the product to be chosen — hence, the performance indica-tors, the standardized assessment, the league tables. The State, regulat-ing the market, insists upon a standardized curriculum and standardized assessments so that rational choices might be exercised. Thus, there is central control, a standard model, and limited choice within a regulated market. What suffers is the recognition of teachers as professionals — that is, as experts within a tradition of liberal education, controlling the agenda and shaping that transaction between teacher and learner within the framework of particular values. No longer can every child count, as those, who handicap the school within the market, come to be excluded. Authority transfers from teacher both to the State, which says what the transaction between teacher and learner is about, and to the parent, which acts as customer in what amounts increasingly to a commercial transaction.

To enable this to happen the language changes. Education becomes a commodity to be bought and sold, the teacher becomes a provider of that commodity and the learner a client, success lies in popularity, the complex struggle of growing understanding is reduced to performance indicators, scholarly and academic judgment is reduced to audits set against systems of quality control. Furthermore, to assist with this qual-ity control the language of measurement has to be thoroughly standard-ized; the attainments are spelt out in terms of behaviours and 'can dos', lists of competencies. The liberal tradition gives way to the language of vocational preparation.

Conclusion

Education is concerned with the transaction which takes place between a teacher and learner. That transaction occurs within a context of beliefs and understandings, of skills and attitudes which are themselves inherited from previous teachers. Education, therefore, depends upon a selective tradition of what is considered worthwhile learning. That tradition picks out certain concepts, ideas, skills, principles. It for ever changes, because that tradition also contains the procedures for and the habit of questioning, subjecting to criticism those very concepts and principles. The educated person has been apprenticed to teachers who introduce him/her to those distinctive ways of experiencing and understanding the world — and to the values and to the procedures through which those ways are constantly examined, criticized and developed through criticism.

Education, conceived as a continual transaction between people, though nonetheless on the basis of a culture which is embodied in books, in texts and in institutions such as universities, might be called liberal for several reasons. It liberates the learners from the ignorance which makes them the victims of whatever power group, politician, fashion-creator competes for their allegiance. It empowers people to think for themselves and to be critical of whatever trivial and half-baked ideas are thrust upon them. It opens up the mind to new ideals and aims worth living for. It both serves and disciplines the imagination.

So valuable and worthwhile, so quintessentially human, is such a view of education, that communities have expected the State to provide the resources to make sure it happens, to preserve that continuity of thinking and criticism and teaching which adds up to a liberal education. At the same time, it has been wary of State interference because the spirit of criticism and of enquiry can so easily be subverted for political ends.

The liberal tradition varies in strength from country to country. Rarely does its spirit completely die. So long as there are men and women with curiosity and an interest in ideas, so there will be teachers willing to impart their enthusiasm and their ideas to others. But it can be stifled. I have suggested four reasons why the State might stifle it. First, powerful people feel that educators themselves have betrayed the liberal tradition — standards therefore need to be redefined by the State. Second, the State questions the efficiency with which its very considerable financial support is being used for education ends. Third, the state wishes to redirect the aim of education towards economic and vocational ends. Fourth, the State fears the consequences of an educated public.

In England and Wales, we have witnessed a massive change since 1944 — a change from the State as the facilitator of a liberal tradition, in which the State would not interfere, to one in which undreamt of powers have now been arrogated to the Secretary of State in determining what should be the content of that educational programme. Such powers seek to control, too, the very nature of teacher training. They are exercised with an arbitrariness that is unprecedented.

To facilitate that, those responsible have developed a system of control through assessment which itself transforms the transaction which takes place between teacher and learner. It requires a very different language from that of liberal education — the language of competencies and behavioural objectives, of performance indicators and audits, of quality assurance and of quality control, of providers and customers, of commodities and of selling. This is the language of management, borrowed from business, the language of State control.

And yet hardly a squeak from the custodians of liberal education.

2 The State, Human Rights and Academic Freedom in Africa

Thandike Mkandawire

Over the years the relationship between the State and African academia has been a complex one and has gone through a number of phases. Post-independence Africa has been characterized by a wide range of authoritarian rule which has encompassed a tantalizing spectrum of ideologies. This rule has either been of the 'one party state' type or military. In all its guises it has severely limited academic freedom in Africa through outright elimination of certain themes or views from national intellectual life, by forcing people into exile, by relegating intellectuals to a realm of numbing silences, by sowing fear through ceaseless intimidation and physical elimination of individuals. Closure of universities has become a regular feature of the African educational landscape.

Although this chapter concentrates on the State and academic freedom, it is my view that repression of academic freedom constitutes only a part of the matrix of the violation of human rights and the web of authoritarian rule in Africa. And while the underlying focus is on academic freedom, we should not be oblivious to the larger question of democratization and human rights in Africa. It is also important to keep in mind that although the State may be the most conspicuous it is not the only culprit. Other elements — civil society, academics, donors etc, can be equally restrictive, and in the final parts of the chapter I touch upon the role of other actors in the violation of academic freedom in Africa. The State's and society's attitudes towards academic freedom are derivative from their overall views of democracy and academic freedom both as practice and as ideological constructs.

The roots of the State's and societal perceptions are both ideational and structural. The first refers to the ideological discourses within which questions of governance, human rights, development, nation-building, tradition and democracy have taken place in Africa. As I shall argue, these discourses have not only provided ideological guidance and nourishment to authoritarian rule, they have also affected responses to it. Among the structural factors we refer to problems of accumulation and the State-society relationships that this has generated or accompanied. I therefore begin by discussing the roots of repressive rule in post-colonial Africa.

Traditional Culture

There have been several attempts to link the quest for democracy, styles of governance and even proclivities towards authoritarian rule to Africa's pre-colonial past. For some authoritarian rule can be traced back to the historical structures and the inherited cultures of Africa. Democracy and the respect for human rights are said to be quintessentially 'Western'. For others, African cultures contain within them seeds of democratic rule and suggest structures of governance most appropriate to Africa. Without getting involved in this not always fruitful debate, we can simply state the following: the African past, like other pasts, contains a wide range of experiences and practices some of which may have a positive bearing on contemporary debates about human rights. Africa was a continent of 'stateless' communities, communalistic democracies, marauding and enslaved communities and nations, and huge empires etc. As such it embodied political practices whose implications for human rights must be considerably varied. In the light of all this, one can make two non-banal observations. In many ways the primordial solidarity ties that have weathered the tides of time have blunted the authoritarian thrust of contemporary central governments and provided protection and solace to populations threatened by slave traders, colonial oppressors and repressive national governments. Another point is that these primordial ties can be so perverted as to be linchpins of intolerance and authoritarian rule. The point here is that what can be extracted from the not always articulate and audible past, depends on the constellation of social forces seeking to read the past, their ideological needs or trajectories and the general levels of consciousness of the population. And as it happens, those who ruled Africa have been able to extract selectively from this past arguments for authoritarian rule. Proverbs of dubious African origin were appealed to justify one man or one party rule or the primacy of collective rights.

Colonial Heritage

Although it is now more than thirty years since Africa's modal year of independence and although any mention of the colonial past is today considered escapist, used by scoundrels blaming everything on others, it is still true that Africa's colonial heritage weighs heavily on both African minds and institutions. This is partly because of the fact that of the institutions that Africa inherited from its colonial masters, the most resilient and the most assiduously cultivated have been the oppressive elements of colonial apparatus — the police, the army, the 'state of emergency' regulations, the intelligence services etc. The disillusionment with African governments combined with a certain 'out of Africa' nostalgia about colonial rule has tended to downplay the repressive nature of colonial rule and to portray it as a much maligned and essentially benevolent operation. Indeed in the popular media an impression is given that colonialism endowed Africa with democratic structures and traditions which for inexplicable reasons Africans have proceeded to squander in the post-independence era. This is patently a false rendition of Africa's modern history. Colonial rule was inherently authoritarian and compulsively repressive since it meant subjugation of one people by another. Colonial 'democratic rule' (as oxymoronic an expression as any) appeared only towards the demise of colonial rule not as a 'natural development' of such rule but as a result of bitter contests which in some cases included armed struggle. It is true that just before granting independence the colonial regimes managed to concoct constitutional arrangements that had all the appearances of the liberal democratic structures of the motherland. However, these structures did not last. In my own country (Malawi) they lasted exactly two months before they were completely abolished with the use of emergency regulations bequeathed us by our erstwhile masters. Not surprisingly, in current debates on democracy whenever the colonial era is evoked it is with respect to the promise of the democratic platforms of the nationalist movements rather than to the colonial heritage. Hence the talk about the 'second independence'.

The issue of academic freedom never rose under colonial rule, which avoided the onerous task of repressing intellectuals by simply producing as few of them as possible. It is, however, noteworthy that the colonial system was extremely uncomfortable with the few it produced. And the best of them were sooner or later to run into trouble — the Kenyattas, the Nkrumahs, the Nehrus.

Post-colonial State

The post-colonial State had a more difficult task than its predecessor. First, the needs of nation-building, the popular demands and the manpower needs of accumulation have compelled the African states dramatically to expand educational opportunities. African governments viewed the new universities with considerable pride and strongly believed that they would serve as agents of development and nation building. This they would do by providing urgently needed manpower, through research and advice to policy-makers and by inculcating certain values and ideologies in the students in their trust.

The general approach to the handling of this vastly larger expansion of the intelligentsia has been conditioned by the general perspectives on governance. The path of governance that has been widely adopted in Africa has been authoritarian. The post colonial African state has not distinguished itself as a great champion of human rights. Indeed gross violation of human rights has been one of the most despicable aspects of post-colonial rule. The main source of the problem was the widespread adoption of authoritarian rule in the form of one-party or military rule. Why this option?

No sooner had the demolition of the short-lived democratic structures been accomplished than a host of theories and justifications for authoritarian rule were advanced. As far as academic freedom was concerned the harbinger of things to come was characteristically signalled by Kwame Nkrumah in the following words:

> We do not intend to sit idly by and see these institutions which are supported by millions of pounds produced out of the sweat and toil of common people continue to be centres of anti-government activities. We want the university college to cease being an alien institution and to take on the character of a Ghanaian University, loyally serving the interest of the nation and the well-being of our people. If reforms do not come from within, we intend to impose them from outside, and no resort to the cry of academic freedom (for academic freedom does not mean irresponsibility) is going to restrain us from seeing that our university is a healthy university devoted to Ghanaian interests. (Cited in Hagan, 1993)

The particular circumstances behind Nkrumah's remarks are discussed by Hagan (1993) and need not detain us here. What is ominous here was that first, Nkrumah was raising an issue that has dogged the State-university relationship ever since — reconciling the State's utilitarian views about universities on the one hand, and the maintenance of standards and the autonomy of universities on the other. This immediately raised the question about the appropriateness of the university models inherited from the metropolitan countries including the vaunted autonomy of universities. It also immediately pitted the university against the State, with members of the former arguing that tinkering with the inherited system would lead to a lowering of standards while the latter argued that exigencies of development and nation-building would demand change.

Nkrumah was also touching on a soft spot of the African intelligentsia. For even within academic circles it was clear that the inherited institutions were somehow at odds with the reality surrounding them not only in terms of material well-being but also in terms of priorities and preoccupations. There was thus considerable soul-searching within universities about the relevance of the institutions, their responsibilities to the less privileged etc. (Mafeje, 1993). Indeed most academics shared the basic ideological tenets informing Nkrumah's threat (nationalism, developmentalism and egalitarianism). And if one adds to the overall ideological congruence, the material comfort and the bright prospects promised by a rapidly expanding civil service and indigenization programmes, one had all the preconditions for harmonious State-academe relationship. And indeed in the early years there was relative peace between the state and academics. From time to time there were altercations on campus but these were largely confined to the material well-being of the community and rarely touched upon the larger societal issues of governance. Generalizing from this period many observers of African politics have sometimes argued that this relative harmony was because the intelligentsia in Africa was itself the recruiting ground for high state functionaries; social analysis for it was therefore uncomfortably close to self-analysis! The academic community was therefore conceived as basically collaborationist and opportunistic. This may be true but it is equally true that academic communities shared the same ideologies as State authorities so that reticence or collaboration were genuine reflections of the intellectuals' acceptance of the 'national project' as adumbrated by the political class. And it is to these that we now turn.

Nationalism and Nation-Building

The first of these was the quest for 'national unity' as an essential element of nation-building. Under this imperative of nation-building nationalism became a totalizing ideology, seeking to bring under its ambit every manifestation of political interest. Some of this fervour for unity was motivated by a genuine desire to rapidly knead together disparate ethnic groups and nationalities into a modern African state. In the event, however, the quest for unity was inadvertently confused with the quest for uniformity. In its less innocent and paranoiac expression, nationalism tended to view political opposition as unpatriotic and divisive. This view was given credence and nourished by the Katanga experience in which political dissension was identified with foreign interference and secessionism — two unforgivable crimes in the demonology of the nationalists. Given such a stance, new states denied themselves the possibilities of dealing with the inherent social pluralism of their societies in a dialogical and non-confrontational manner. Every articulation of genuine local interests, or manifestation of ethnic identity was viewed as almost treasonous and was harshly suppressed.

Another issue related to differences about rights and the values attached to them. More specifically, there was the question of choice between collective and individual rights. In the early post-independence years the stress by both states and intellectuals was on collective rights. For historical reasons this has been the main emphasis within Africa and is still stressed by some (Shivji, 1989). One reason for this bias was the continued importance of the struggle against imperialism and racial domination in Africa. To the extent that both these denied a whole people their right to self-determination they could not but be the central focus of African discourse. Individual rights appeared secondary to these larger rights. Indeed it was argued that the pre-conditions of the exercise of individual rights was the attainment of collective rights such as self-determination. However, although self-determination was undoubtedly necessary, it did not always lead to the enjoyment of basic human rights as enshrined in the UN Charter and other documents to which African countries had been signatories. The nationalist movement which had ably used the clauses on collective rights in the various international conventions to make their case were usually not able to go beyond those rights. And indeed once in power, they were to so stress the dichotomy between collective and individual rights as to suggest that while the former were somehow African, the latter were definitely foreign. The African debate also stressed responsibilities that went with rights. To compound matters there were other 'rights' (for example, rights to development) that were juxtaposed with the list of conventional human rights in a manner that gave the false impression that somehow these rights were in conflict.

Nationalism and its rhetoric and proclamations were difficult to contend with. First, in the early years the triumphant nationalists, armed with impeccable testimonies to their personal commitment to the nation (many years in exile or detention) stood on very high moral ground and indeed, could, with some justification, claim they spoke for the nation when they chastised academics for abusing academic freedom by engaging in trivial pursuits which did not address the urgent tasks of nation-building and development. Second, the nationalists demonstrated their commitment to university education and their genuine belief that universities would produce the manpower that was required for development by funding the universities rather lavishly, at least when compared to the miserable allocations to African universities today. Third, African universities were cursed by their parentage which made them easily suspect in the eyes of the nationalists. Most of the universities were modelled after similar institutions in metropolitan countries and were initially staffed by expatriates. This genesis made them vulnerable to charges that their opposition to the nationalists' agenda was a reflection of their alien character or worse their 'colonial mentality' which made them a 'veritable breeding ground of unpatriotic and anti-government elements' to use Nkrumah's characterization of the university college (cited in Hagan, 1993). Fourth, academics themselves shared the nationalist ideology and aspirations. African intellectuals and statesmen contributed to the construction of this ideological edifice of authoritarian rule. Various particularistic ideologies were advanced — African socialism, Marxist-Leninism, authenticity, African humanism, Nkrumahism etc. All these ideologies tended to argue for one party rule either because this was what our heritage recommended, or because it was scientific or because it was the only way to establish national unity and ensure development.

Developmentalism

A second source of authoritarian rule was the 'modernization' and 'developmentalist' ideology which tended to subject every other value to its own peculiar and unrelenting exigencies. According to its precepts, development needed national unity; it needed foreign investment which in turn needed discipline and docile labour; it needed a singleness of purpose so that the ambivalences and compromises inherent in democracy were luxuries that would have to await the attainment of 'development'. One party or authoritarian rule would curtail 'decision costs' incurred through democratic decision-making procedures (Rothchild and Curry, 1978). This development discourse was so pervasive and so much part of conventional wisdom in both African and donor countries that it permitted the most extensive violation of human rights to occur as long as 'development' was somehow taking place. Indeed high rates of economic growth and political stability were considered enough justification for the violation of human rights. Development was 'no easy task' and it required a hard-headedness that condoned violation of human rights as long as a brighter future was being extolled. The main slogan of this position could have been 'Silence: Development in progress'. If democracy was to be placed on the agenda at all, it had to demonstrate that it was promotive of development, or at least, was compatible with it.

Here again African intellectuals were in a vulnerable position. The visceral populism of most African intellectuals tended to persuade them to accept this option, albeit grudgingly. In the 'developmentalist' logic it always appeared immoral to ask for freedom to think and express oneself when such elementary freedoms as freedom to eat were denied.

Ake (1993) posed the question quite sharply:

> . . . why should we care about academic freedom in Africa? It is difficult enough to justify the demand for political freedom where limitation of poverty, illiteracy and poor health and the rigour of the daily struggle seem to demand entirely different priorities. It is difficult still to defend the demand for academic freedom which is a very special kind of bourgeois freedom limited to a very small group. Why do we think we are entitled to demand academic freedom and why do we think that our demand deserves to be upheld by the rest of society?

It is a question that still haunts African intellectuals[1]. It is also a point that repressive governments have raised against academics sometimes with devastating effects when the public has become hostile to academics. This bred a disarming ambiguity among African academics about the relationship between academic freedom and their social responsibility, an ambiguity that has been a source of much soul-searching by a community whose populist bent has cast doubt on the priority of academic freedom when other such 'basic freedoms' (as the right to food, shelter and education) are denied to so many of their compatriots.

I think it is important to bear in mind how the developmentalist exigencies have played havoc on human rights in Africa. For today we are once again faced with the arguments that the exigencies of the economy — in this case structural adjustment — demand states that have the 'political will' (read military capacity) to implement these policies unencumbered by the democratic demands of domestic forces and that defence of academic institutions is tantamount to 'rent seeking' by the academic establishment not ready to subject its cloistered life to the logic of the market.

The Nature of the State and Development

However more significant than these ideological underpinnings of the intolerance of the African state, was the character of the state itself. I will not enter into the tortuous debate on the nature and character of the State. One outstanding feature of the post-independence African State was its reach and its pervasive presence in all walks of life. Its tentacles extended not only to all sectors of the economy but to every nook and cranny of civil society. The ubiquity of the State meant that it was loathed and courted at the same time. It led to insecurity, paranoia, self-censorship, opportunism and sycophancy among those who sought access to State patronage (Ake, 1993; Diouf and Mamdani, 1993). With the State looming so large it is no surprise that this led to statist perceptions of social transformation among African intellectuals by obscuring or overshadowing other social actors for which they have been severely criticized (Diouf and Mamdani, 1993). Another characteristic of the State was its dependency on or weakness vis à vis foreign powers. This gave a high premium to the views of foreign powers on such things as human rights and academic freedom, a fact that has been underscored by the current practice of 'political conditionality'.

Another critical factor affecting human rights was the model of development adopted by most African governments. Although in the early years of independence rapid expansion in social services and indigenization of the civil services did much to reduce the inequalities bred by colonial rule, the development strategy adopted tended to engender processes of income distribution that were inherently sources of conflict. These developments were to intensify processes of social differentiation which the blanket of discrimination by colonial rulers against all natives had artificially blocked and were to put strains on the nationalist coalition created during the struggle for independence. Governments were increasingly forced to rely more on coercion than consensus.

Although themselves beneficiaries of these processes, academics were among the first to point to the problematic nature of the emerging class differentiation and social stratification. They also criticized the growing malaise of corruption and the illicit enrichment that the state was nurturing. However, as noted above, this criticism seemed to be circumscribed by the ideological parameters these intellectuals shared with the state authorities.

Things were made worse by the crisis of the early 1970s and the 80s. Following first the 'oil crisis' and later, the fall in terms of trade of primary commodities, the recession in the developed countries, high interest on a rapidly mounting debt and gross mismanagement, African economies were in a shambles by the end of the 1970s. Most African governments entered into some form of agreement with the IMF and World Bank which insisted on the adoption of structural adjustments that called for severe austerity. With state coffers empty, African states had no resources to maintain the precarious coalition that had hitherto sustained some modicum of legitimacy to existing governments. With no carrots left, governments were left with sticks as the major means of persuasion. The 1980s saw a dramatic increase in the violation of human rights. Academic freedom was not spared in this wave of economic liberalism and political repression. First, the standing of the university was undermined by the World Bank's suggestion that the rate of return of university education was low as compared to primary and secondary education. The message was that governments should drastically curtail expenditure on higher education or even close down some of the institutions or faculties. Although most African governments (ministries of education) rejected the dubious calculus behind such assertions, the economic downgrading of universities gave the ministers of finance a strong argument for starving universities. This led to the rapid degradation of living, teaching and research conditions in the universities.

The initial reaction of academics was to oppose the cuts and the introduction of 'cost-recovering' measures that the Bretton Woods institution was pushing. As the crisis deepened, academics turned their anger against structural adjustment programmes as a whole and eventually to the forms of governance that had led to the crisis and that had accepted imposed packages without consulting the general republic. It is this that explains the combination of opposition to structural adjustment and the calls for democratization and accountability.

To compound matters further was the decision by the World Bank to step into the funding of higher education. True to logic, the Bank sought 'bankable' activities within the university. In the most flagrant flexing of its financial muscle, in Nigeria the Bank went as far as to insist on looking at curricula and vetting book orders for Nigerian universities apparently to make sure that the chosen discipline had the requisite rates of return and that the books ordered were inputs in these profitable exercises. To the Bank's surprise, there was widespread protest from the academic community which, although severely starved of funds, saw the Bank's programme as crude interference with university autonomy and destruction of university life.

Other Actors

One-sided discussion of academic freedom tends to place the entire blame on State structures. However, the Kampala Conference recognized and paid considerable attention to the role of other actors, including donors, the intellectuals (domestic and foreign) and civil society.

The Donors and Academic Freedom

Foreign donors play an important role in Africa. Their presence provides opportunities and raises a number of questions. On the one hand, the presence of external funding has enormously expanded the space for social science research in Africa. It is clear that in a number of research fields only their presence has made research possible. And indeed in a number of countries, the only funds available for research are foreign, inflation and devaluation having reduced the nominal allocation of domestic funds to these activities to naught. In addition, by being free from a number of domestic political constraints, foreign donors have been able to fund research themes that no local authority would dare. Furthermore, the high moral standing of some of the donors has shielded grantees from repressive measures by local authorities.

On the other hand, foreign funding brings with it its own constraints. First, the substantial contributions it is making to social research has given the donor community inordinate power with consequent intended or unintended constraints on social science research. These can and do take a variety of forms. By giving priority to project over programme or by putting the emphasis on consultancy rather than research or funding they can shape the research agenda. Donors can eliminate work in certain areas by merely indicating which areas they consider fundable. They can by their explicit or implicit ideological preferences, nurture forms of self-censorship among researchers desperate for funding. Research may be constrained by bureaucratization of evaluation procedures where 'doability' narrows the areas that can be safely funded to meet certain bureaucratic schedules and goals. These pressures often express themselves through over burdened programme officers who must evaluate a very wide range of research activities in a not always familiar environment. The penury of the research community in which they work places them in a situation in which it is tempting to pull strings (Mkandawire, 1993). The shifts in donor interests have much wider implications for continuity and accumulative prospects of African research than donor and even recipients may be fully aware of.

Donors operate within the same African political environment. In some cases research funding may be part of intimate interstate relationships that may prevent the use of funds for research ideas that are deemed not compatible with these more privileged interstate relationships. It should be pointed out that while they may be relatively free from the political constraint of the recipient country, they are accountable to public or private authorities in their respective countries. Such accountability may not always permit funding of certain forms of research or themes (Khan, 1993).

In addition, donors were also enmeshed in the developmentalist ideology. It was thus in the name of developmentalism that the outside world accepted repressive regimes. It is only quite recently that the Bandas and Houpheit-Boignys were said to be writing 'success stories'. One effect was that donors tended to consider debates on academic freedom as just that — academic, and the complaining academics were listened to with the indulgence reserved for a precocious child-making mistakes.

To this ideological bias, one must add the Cold War which tended to colour donors' views of particular regimes. Africa attained its independence under the atomic shadow of the Cold War. This was to have profound implications on the international context of state formation and nation building in Africa. While the Cold War facilitated the struggle against colonial rule, it also allowed for forms of clientelism that condoned or encouraged forms of governance that were not respectful of human rights as long as the regimes served the geopolitical interest of the patron power. Struggles for human rights or democracy or development were subordinated to the imperatives of superpower struggles. It does not matter what a particular bastard did as long as he/she was 'our bastard', to paraphrase an American General's excuse for supporting the Saigon Regime. Assured of this protection a number of client states didn't even bother to cultivate a modicum of legitimacy at the national level. Reduced to the status of occupying armies they could massively and impudently violate the human and democratic rights of their people fully confident that the financial and arms flow would not be impaired by their misconduct.

The Intelligentsia and Academic Freedom

Although both the corporate interests and ideological predispositions of African intellectuals gradually and ineluctably pushed them to the forefront of struggles for human rights and academic freedom, the structures dominated by researchers and the intelligentsia themselves are far from unproblematic. Nor were their practices and attitudes always conducive to an open research milieu. Inherited traditions, dogmatic disposition, hierarchical and authoritarian research structures and traditions, intolerance or discriminations on intellectual, ethnic, gender or religious basis and corruption have, alas, made their presence in African universities (Ayesha, 1993; Mazrui, 1993). If one adds to this the opportunism that turned some academics into state informants or sycophants, it becomes clear that candid discussion of these problems is essential if the critique by African researchers of others' practices is to be morally justifiable, or at least credible.

Foreign Colleagues and Academic Freedom

One issue that was raised by both the African and non-African participants at the Kampala Symposium on Academic Freedom was the role of non-African academics in all this. Most non-Africans addressing themselves on human rights in Africa were initially intimidated by the charges that they were imposing on Africa individualistic conceptions of rights that were Eurocentric, or that they were skirting the issues of violation of collective rights by imperialism or racism or that if they were serious about human rights they ought to ensure enough transfer of resources to buttress the 'right to development'. Solidarity from outside did not only have to contend with this official view of things but lacked clearly identified social movements with which to work in solidarity. Part of this was due to genuine ignorance about or actual absence of counterparts in Africa. However, some of it stemmed from the paternalism that many NGOs in the 'North' have yet to rid themselves of and which blinded them from seeing local efforts.

There was bitterness at the passivity and even complicity of foreign academics. The desire to get one's research done and the need for research permits and institutional affiliation had led to behaviour by non-African colleagues that was not supportive of struggles for democracy in Africa. There were examples of fraternisation with repressive regimes that seemed to go beyond the need for information for research. The sight of a major scholar one has admired so much ingratiating a dictator was disheartening. African regimes exploited this very well. They could turn to their public and show how prominent scholars accepted them while their local yelping intellectuals criticized them.

A number of African governments felt they could arrest or force their nationals into exile fully confident that they could always find expatriates less troublesome than indigenous scholars.

Civil Society and Freedom of Research in Africa

Although much of the debate on academic freedom tends to confine itself to the confrontations of the state and the academic, it is clear that the status of academic freedom within civil society, the relationship between the state and civil society as a whole, the level of political consciousness and the values attached to academic freedom profoundly affect prospects of academic freedom. Indeed it is difficult to imagine academic freedom that is not attached to the larger democratic gains by the civil society.

It is currently popular to depict State-civil relationships in manichean terms: State bad — civil society good. The Kampala Conference clearly established that such a view was too simplistic. Civil society can and does impose its own contraints on research usually through biases of a sociocultural nature. An example of this would be restrictions on study of gender issues (Imam and Ayesha, 1993; Mazrui, 1993), critical evaluations of certain social movements such as religious movements etc. (Mazrui, 1993). Contributing to all this may be the low status of the social scientists whose research activities civil society may associate with state security investigations or tax collection or simply prying into the privacy of individuals or households.

One of the responses to the current crisis has been the rise of religious fundamentalism. In some countries this has led to greater intolerance of what is going on in the universities. In Algeria, academics have simply been murdered by religious death squads and a number of academics are in hiding not from the state but from religious groups.

The New Wave of Democratization

The last few years have witnessed important struggles against authoritarian rule. The struggles are unprecedented and far-ranging and reminiscent of the days of the struggle for independence. A number of authoritarian regimes have collapsed or been transformed. For the first time since independence a number of countries are ruled by democratically-elected leaders.

Although Africa has been influenced by the wave of democratization engulfing the world and benefitted from solidarity contributions from outside Africa, the main impetus is essentially African. While perhaps not making much economic progress, Africa has undergone significant social change. The levels of literacy have increased dramatically since independence; rates of urbanization have accelerated rapidly so that in some countries (Zambia and Congo) urban populations exceeded rural populations; technology has given access to information to large number of people despite government censorship. Africans knew more about struggles for democracy and human rights not only in neighbouring countries but worldwide. In Africa, the struggles of children of Soweto and Mandela's heroic pronouncements from Robben Island have inspired a whole generation of youth.

In addition, the economic crisis has brought into sharp focus the blight of corruption, the inequities of the economy and the widespread mismanagement of national resources. It has also brought to light the extent of foreign intervention in national affairs and the fragility of national sovereignty. These factors have activated a wide range of social forces against authoritarian regimes.

These struggles have radically reshaped debates on human rights and academic freedom. The approach to human rights and academic freedom in the 1970–80s did not address itself to the question of democracy. Concentrating on the exposure of individual cases of violation of human rights this approach tended to shy away from problems of governance and power relations in society. It often failed to contextualize the violation of human rights. More specifically, it rarely sought to link human rights to struggles for democratization. This absence of context tended to lend a quixotic air to the various protests against the violation of human rights in certain countries. It also tended to focus attention on individual cases whose resolution would often disrupt solidarity movements by giving them a false sense of success.

Even more pertinent to our discussion is the extent to which the academic community now takes its own rights seriously and is less disposed to accept the alleged trade-off between its rights and the well being of the poor or of the nation. As the intelligentsia has become detached from ruling circles, and as its own conditions have tended to share in the adversity being experienced by the wider society, intellectuals have organized to protect their corporate interests, both financial (salary, benefits) and otherwise (autonomy of work). Academic staff associations and student unions have developed on numerous campuses and have played a central role in the current struggles for democratization. Paradoxically, in a large number of cases, the intensification of struggles for democratization and the subsequent widening of political space for society at large has worsened the relationship between the State and academics. The new atmosphere has encouraged large numbers of academics to participate in national debates more openly and more defiantly than ever before. The abandonment of self-censorship and the emergence from clandestine intellectual activities by many academics has exposed them to direct and open confrontation with the beleaguered state which views them as the direct source of public protest against authoritarian rule. Accustomed to the graveyard silence it has imposed on virtually all elements of society, the African state has taken even the most benign expressions of discontent as subversive or seditious. Not surprisingly, the closure of universities, the prohibition of professional and student associations, the incarceration and even outright assassinations of individuals have increased at precisely the time when the 'African Spring' seems visible.

The Tasks Ahead

Although reports by the foreign press and economists that the democratization processes have come to a sudden halt in Africa are highly exaggerated, the processes of democratization are not moving as smoothly as they should be. There are still many obstacles — internal and external. As I write now, many universities in Africa are closed. Apparently, governments believe that closure of universities is less politically onerous than detaining individual academics.

Internal Obstacles

Among the internal obstacles, the main one is the resistance of the authoritarian structures themselves. Compelled by both internal and external pressures to democratize, most of the authoritarian rulers are assiduously trying to outmanoeuvre the democratic forces and hoodwink the rest of the world. They hold rigged elections (Cameroon); they still continue to monopolize the use of force through their hold over the praetorian guards and constantly nullify democratic processes through intimidation. (Togo is a classic case in point.) They so truncate the electoral processes and so load them against the opposition (control the media, set up legal barriers to meetings, abuse state infrastructure for personal electoral purposes) as to make their victories a foregone conclusion — Ghana is one such example. They conduct electoral charades for foreign observers who have no idea of the politics, the geography, the local administration or logistical capacities of the state. In the worst case, they go through the whole electoral processes only to reject the results when they are unpalatable to them. Nigeria has undergone such a painful hoax.

In addition to the oppressive activities of state structures, there are the weaknesses of political opposition from civil society. Although Africa is a continent of vibrant associational life, it is only in recent years that this life has translated itself into effective political activities. The weakness of social movements have many explanations and the study of social movements in Africa is one of the new areas of interest. One source has been the repressive conditions under which any movements in African have to operate under the shadow of the all-engulfing State or party. In addition the social pluralism of Africa has been manipulated so as to undermine broad-based, trans-ethnic movements. In addition, Africa is the least urbanized continent. This is in a situation in which the peculiar African agrarian structure is not conducive to the 'peasant movements' that have such important roles in Asian and Latin American societies.

One should add here that not all protest against existing authoritarian regimes is or has been democratic in form let alone in substance. In significant cases this protest has assumed religious fundamentalist forms or ethnic irredentist expressions that are not conducive to democratization. These new democratic movements and processes which they have unleashed need close observation and critical appraisal.

External Obstacles

The external obstacles are related to the nature of the economic crisis facing African countries and the nature of structural adjustment programmes being imposed by the international financial system. Ever since the 'oil crisis' of 1973 and even more so after the second oil crisis of 1979, most African countries have witnessed drastic declines in their economy. To solve their problems, most of them (thirty-three at the last count) have entered into agreements with the IMF and World Bank for assistance. These institutions have imposed a standard package of austerity which has included drastic cuts in government expenditure, devaluation of national currencies, liberalization of the trade regime, privatization of the economy and a tight monetary policy. There is still great controversy about the appropriateness of these policies for African conditions and the diagnosis underlying their prescription. There is still considerable debate about their effects. Suffice it to note the following: (i) the measures have contributed to the worsening of living standards. This was expected even by their advocates. The downturn was supposed to constitute the 'vale of tears' that African countries would have to traverse before neo-liberal salvation was bestowed on the continent; (ii) most of the politically active groups have opposed these measures; (iii) a number of the 'favourite students' of the international finance institutions have been military rulers who have been able to impose these measures unencumbered by domestic debates; (iv) the new democratic regimes are being forced to implement these measure which may undermine the legitimacy and compromise the entire process of democratization; (v) the international institutions devising and dictating economic policy in Africa are neither transparent nor accountable to local political processes. Their calls for transparency, popular participation and accountability stand in obscene contrast with their arrogance, secrecy and undemocratic conduct. Indeed in most cases, they either hijack key economic decision-making centres or deprive them of any meaningful influence; (vi) there has been an unwarranted conflation of economic liberalization with political democratization by key funding institutions, even though in Africa, as elsewhere, there is the real possibility of the liberalization of the market being accompanied by the fettering of the polity.

Democracy without Tears

I have suggested how negatively the 'developmentalist' ideology has tended to impact upon human rights and academic freedom and how the State has legitimized its repressive policies by appealing to its putative exigencies. This should, however, not be construed as to suggest that development in the sense of improvement in the material living standards of the people is not important, and even less that it is inimical to people's exercise of human rights. A democratic structure in which the majority of the population was too enfeebled by poverty, too blinded by illiteracy and too debilitated by the ravages of disease to meaningfully participate in the democratic processes would be a cruel hoax. Development is therefore still on the agenda and should be a concern for all democratic forces. The debate on human rights, academic and democratic, will therefore have to address itself to the problems of underdevelopment and inequity. We should struggle for a 'democracy without tears', a democracy which guarantees every individual the opportunity to develop their capacity to as high a level as is materially possible, and which provides every individual the material and social wherewithall to exercise his/her democratic rights.

Note

1   This is clearly illustrated by the high value given to 'social responsibility' in the Kampala Declaration on Academic Freedom. It is also echoed in a

number of presentations at the conference. See especially Ake (1993), Diouf Mamdani (1993) and Mafeje (1993).

References

AFRICA WATCH (1991) *Academic Freedom and Human Rights Abuses in Africa*, New York, Human Rights Watch.

AKE, C. (1993) 'Academic freedom and material base', in DIOUF, M. and MAMDANI, M. (Eds) *Academic Freedom in Africa*, Dakar, CODESRIA.

BAKO, S. (1993) 'Education and adjustment in Nigeria: Conditionality and resistance', in DIOUF, M. and MAMDANI, M. (Eds) *Academic Freedom in Africa*, Dakar, CODESRIA.

HAGAN, G. (1993) 'Academic freedom and national responsibility in an African state', in DIOUF, M. and MAMDANI, M. (Eds) *Academic Freedom in Africa*, Dakar, CODESRIA.

HYDEN, G. (1991) 'The efforts to restore intellectual freedom in Africa', *A Journal of Opinion*, XX/1.

IMAM and AMINA (1993) 'The role of academics in limiting and expanding academic freedom', in DIOUF, M. and MAMDANI, M. (Eds) *Academic Freedom in Africa*, Dakar, CODESRIA.

KHAN, A. (1993) 'Algerian intellectuals: Between identity and modernity', in DIOUF, M. and MAMDANI, M. (Eds) *Academic Freedom in Africa*, Dakar, CODESRIA.

MAFEJE, A. (1993) 'Beyond academic freedom: The struggle for authenticity in African social science discourse', in DIOUF, M. and MAMDANI, M. (Eds) *Academic Freedom in Africa*, Dakar, CODESRIA.

MAZRUI, A. (1993) 'The impact of global changes on academic freedom in Africa: A preliminary assessment', in DIOUF, M. and MAMDANI, M. (Eds) *Academic Freedom in Africa*, Dakar, CODESRIA.

MKANDAWIRE, T. (1993) 'Problems and prospects of social sciences in Africa', *International Social Science Journal*, February, pp. 129–40.

ROTHCHILD, D. and CURRY, R. (1978) *Scarcity, Choice and Public Policy in Middle Africa*, London, University of California Press.

SHIVJI, I. (1989) *The Concept of Human Rights in Africa*, Dakar, CODESRIA.

3   Educational Contestability and the Role of the State

Geoffrey Partington

Contestability

Contemporary liberal-democratic states have in essence a choice between three roles in the promotion of education. The first is to require that parents ensure their children are in situations deemed educational either for a given number of years or until certain stipulated levels of attainment have been achieved, but to refrain from providing education except when non-governmental provision is unavailable. This is comparable to policies most contemporary liberal democracies pursue in respect of children's physical welfare: parents are vulnerable to prosecution for neglect unless they feed their children, but the State does not act as baker or butcher or fishmonger. Priority to parents was the position of John Stuart Mill, who deprecated the idea that 'the whole or any part of the education of the people should be in State hands' and explained:

> If the government would make up its mind to require for every child a good education, it might save itself the trouble of providing one. It might leave to parents to obtain the education where and how they pleased, and content itself with helping to pay the school fees of the poorer classes of children, and defraying the entire school expenses of those who have no one else to pay for them . . . A general State education is a mere contrivance for moulding people to be exactly like one another: and as the mould in which it casts them is that which pleases the predominant power in the government, whether this be a monarch, a priesthood, an aristocracy, or the majority of the existing generation, in proportion as it is efficient and successful, it establishes a despotism over the mind. (Mill, 1910, p. 161)

The second is to provide as well as require education but to leave matters of curriculum, pedagogy and accreditation of standards largely to professional experts. Power over education swung to the experts in several English-speaking countries during the 1970s and 1980s, until alleged weaknesses in their prescriptions led to renewed governmental restrictions on professional autonomy. The third is for governments to control curriculum, pedagogy and accreditation in the light of their own perceptions of national needs. Mass education was developed first in Prussia and the Netherlands under close State direction. Twentieth century totalitarian states intensified this control to previously unknown degrees but even in contemporary liberal democracies powerful and influential groups are attracted, at least when a favourable ministry is in office, to extensive governmental control over education.

Irrespective of the locus of decision-making, parental, professional or governmental, there are bound to be far-reaching contests about educational priorities in pluralist and open societies, since educational values are inherently contestable (Gallie, 1968). The contestable must be differentiated from the arbitrary or subjective as well as the dogmatic; many statements and claims can be demonstrated to be factually mistaken, conceptually incoherent or fatally flawed in some other non-arbitrary way; and every educational theory and practice may be improved in the light of informed debate and relevant evidence. Yet legitimate disagreements about values priorities persist after every possible semantic and factual clarification has been made. Educational theories may be reduced to five distinctive clusters in terms of the highest category of priority advanced by each one:

(i)   Instrumentalist: needs of the existing society.
(ii) Radical-reconstructionist: creation of a different and better society.
(iii) Transcendental: salvation or initiation into religious faith.
(iv) Child-centred: needs of children.
(v)   Liberal: knowledge deemed of greatest intrinsic value.

Attempts in heterogenous Western democracies such as the USA, England, Australia and Canada to create what Mark Holmes (1992) terms 'low doctrine' public school systems, minimally disturbing to all educational beliefs, have made it very difficult for schools to foster or transmit any coherent set of positive values. On the other hand governmental attempts in the name of political correctness to enforce a single political doctrine creates understandable resentment. In any case, despite misleading rhetoric, no Western democracy has a common comprehensive school system, since in each there is a large sector of schools not provided or directly controlled by governmental bodies. Financial treatment of non-Government schools is highly variable: funding is available in England for Anglican and Roman Catholic but not Moslem schools, in Ontario for Roman Catholic and Chinese language schools but not Protestant ones, and in Massachusetts for numerous alternative schools but not for the religious-based schools attended by huge numbers of Roman Catholics and other Christians. In Australia some of the most vociferous enemies of all other forms of Government support for non-Government schools are enthusiastic advocates of fully-funded schools for Aborigines based on traditional 'Dreamtime' beliefs.

Disappointed Hopes

During the 1950s and 1960s in countries such as Britain, a broad if informal coalition existed in favour of rapid Government-funded educational expansion. The most fashionable version of instrumentalism, human capital theory, was highly optimistic about the correlation of years spent in education, class size and other aspects of input with economic progress through the achievement of higher educational standards. Theorists such as Schultz (1961) and Becker (1962) believed the proportion of young people in education would always show a high positive correlation with economic efficiency and industrial productivity, almost irrespective of the effort students made or the quality and appropriateness of their instruction. Some advocates of liberal education such as Geoffrey Bantock and Kingsley Amis feared that rapid expansion would undermine, rather than strengthen, academic standards, but others were sanguine that a good general education could successfully be extended to a much wider proportion of young people than in the past. The main thrust in early campaigns for comprehensive education in Britain was to extend the more demanding curricula of the selective schools to the mass of children. Child-centred educators were in general enthusiastic for educational expansion, provided that 'alternative education' of various forms was available, within as well as outside the range of state provision. Many religiously oriented schools and transcendentalist educators considered expansion propitious to their aims and purposes and were content to accept more Government direction than in the past. Despite theoretical misgivings about the nature of the capitalist state, radical reconstructionists were the most vociferous advocates of rapid expansion in state education.

Optimism about the power of education led to unprecedented public funding, improved pupil-teacher ratios, longer pre-service teacher education etc. In every Australian state, for example, real *per capita* expenditure on both primary and secondary students almost doubled each decade after 1960. Over the last two decades, however, there has been reduced confidence that greater investment in education almost automatically results in higher educational achievement, which, in its turn necessarily leads to greater national efficiency (or more social 'equity' or other aims and purposes). There remains a significant gap in most advanced economies between the salaries of university graduates and people of lower formal qualifications and this gap actually widened in the United States between 1979 and 1987 (Commission on the Skills of the American Workforce, 1990), but only a weak relationship has been detected over the last two decades between educational expenditure and retention rates on the one hand and industrial productivity and economic efficiency on the other. Maglen *et al* (1994) observe on the contemporary Australian scene

> Despite the constant affirmation of the important role that education and training play in the economic success of individuals, enterprises and nations, there is much uncertainty about the likely pay-off from any additional investment in education and training . . . The case for educational investment is not helped by the fact that the increased educational attainment of the Australian labour force over the past 20 years does not appear to have been associated with any marked rise in labour productivity. (p. 1)

Liberal expectations of a wider public for good literature, music and art were not only weakly fulfilled at best, but a philistine counter-culture seemed to flourish all the more as numbers in full-time education increased. Other anticipated goods proved elusive: increased sex education did not seem to promote sexual health and happiness among young people and courses to reduce smoking, drinking, drugs, seemed largely ineffective. The incidence of such ills might, of course, have been even higher had there been no courses designed to combat them, and no educational expansion, but evidence for the positive effects of school programs is very sparse.

Radical-Reconstruction and the State

The forms of radical reconstructionism which gained greatest influence from the mid-1960s until the late 1980s were neo-Marxist in character, even though Marxism in its Stalinist and Maoist forms suffered a major setback during those years. Marxism in virtually all its varieties exhibits deep internal contradictions in respect of the relationship of State and education. Marx himself, notably in his 1875 *Critique of the Gotha Program*, sometimes warned against extending the power of the capitalist State over education, but in day-to-day politics in England he generally favoured the extension of compulsory elementary education under governmental auspices. Contemporary neo-Marxists have even more deeply split minds, believing with Althusser that educational institutions form part of an Ideological State Apparatus designed to strengthen the power of ruling-class ideas, so that further extensions of State intervention in education should be resisted or at least viewed with deep suspicion, yet ardently and uncritically supporting such extensions and strongly hostile to private education and choice within state education. Two Australian neo-Marxist sociologists (Branson and Miller, 1979) claimed

> The whole education system operates to ensure that inequalities fundamental to capitalist production — in particular those based on class and sex — are constantly being reproduced. Social stratification in Australia does not exist despite the provision of 'free, secular and compulsory' schooling, but because of it. (p. 2)

Although the advanced capitalist state was held to provide ideological support for capitalist (and/or patriarchal/homophobic/white) interests, it was evidently through the power of the state that capitalism and/or patriarchy/homophobia/white supremacy was to be overthrown by the progressive forces, led by neo-Marxist academics. It was painful after 1979 for radical-reconstructionists in Britain to confront an unfriendly Government in Westminster, yet the pain made it relatively easier to maintain Althusserian delusions. For many Antipodean radicals their own elevation to commanding heights of power in educational bureaucracies, universities and teacher unions during the post-1983 ALP ascendancy posed sharper theoretical problems. Australia was still a capitalist state, since the revolution had not yet taken place, yet radical-reconstructionists were the decision makers in education and met little resistance to syllabuses denouncing Australia as racist, sexist and generally oppressive. Perhaps radicals themselves were unknowing instruments of concealed ruling class interests which cunningly deployed techniques of repressive tolerance and incorporation, as Marcuse once warned? Feminist equal opportunities advisers had a similar problem, since they believed the system under which they exerted authority remained patriarchal and oppressive.

As in Britain during the seventies radical-reconstruction was adapted in Australia during the 1980s to suit the interests of professional educators. Broad agreement was achieved with some child-centred educators that the most valuable curriculum is based on the actual lives and felt interests of students, although an unfortunate consequence was that the most culturally deprived children were then likely to receive least intellectual stimulus in their schools. Teachers themselves, of course, actually determined what was truly relevant and significant in children's experiences and what on the contrary was evidence of false consciousness induced by a racist, patriarchal, capitalist society. Claims about happiness and creativity were readily incorporated, since unhappiness could always be attributed to external conditions, particularly to unsatisfactory parents and an unjust society, and since teachers were sole judges of whether their students' work was creative, innovatory, caring or critical. Child-centred theories which actually vest authority in individual children or peer-groups and thus may lead to an expansion of educational choice were spurned.

The Marxism of Marx and Lenin was epistemologically materialist and objectivist but neo-Marxism is highly relativistic and espouses postmodernist theories such as structuralism and deconstructionism. Neo-Marxism rejects subject disciplines as merely arbitrary constructs and derides the very concepts of objective standards of excellence or canons of exemplary past achievements or intrinsically valuable knowledge. It deplores the exclusion of allegedly disadvantaged groups from the cultural capital of the privileged, but nobody is genuinely disadvantaged educationally by being excluded from cultural capital if it is merely the ideology of the ruling class. Neo-Marxists, such as Professor Kevin Harris of the University of New South Wales, argue, not merely that education has a political dimension, which is a truism, but is utterly political, since 'there cannot be a-political knowledge about anything' (Harris, 1988, p. 34). Thus it would be ridiculous to complain of radical politicization of the curriculum. Yet, once elected liberal-conservative governments challenged, albeit very timidly, radical ideology in education, they were accused by radicals of vile and unprecedented political interference with schools hitherto innocent of political purpose or intent.

Information about Educational Standards

During the pre-Thatcher years in Britain many radical-reconstructionists and child-centred educators supported forms of core or National Curriculum, since they were shaping them. Even then, however, there was strong opposition to testing or assessment which might expose teachers, schools or school systems to criticism. The advent of the Conservatives to Government in 1979 was followed by intensive education industry resistance to testing, but the Tories succeeded in enacting legislation such as the 1989 Education Act which made available to the public information about the overall academic achievement of each school. In Australia during most of the eighties educational radicalism exerted great influence over ALP governments and not only resisted any new testing but succeeded in reducing public information at virtually every level from the kindergarten to the university. A wide range of arguments was deployed to this end.

One objection to assessment and especially to dissemination of its results was that information about educational achievement is open to manipulation and abuse, especially to unfair and odious comparisons. Information, however reliable and relevant it may be, is always, of course, capable of being misused, but this ever-present danger is hardly sufficient grounds for failing to obtain appropriate information or for suppressing it when it is available. The odious comparison which most incensed Australian teacher unions and state educational bureaucracies was that between school systems. The last national tests of literacy and numeracy (in 1976 and 1981) in Australia which published relevant data disclosed disparities in favour of non-Government schools, such as (Keeves and Bourke, 1976, pp. 98–9): 'In general, at the 10 year old level the students in the Independent schools performed above the students in the Catholic and Government schools'. Background variables over which schools have no control may, of course, have been responsible for such disparities. Educators seriously concerned about standards of educational achievement would have eagerly supported research into this and other possible explanations, but there was instead a determination to prevent any such inquiries in future.

A second objection has been that assessment of standards damages students' self-esteem. On this view children with high self-esteem forge ahead academically, but those with low self-esteem fall behind. Person-to-person criticism of any efforts by students is bad enough, but any sort of wider or more public assessment which contains a significant possibility of failure is anathema. Some teachers who imagined themselves to be liberators of oppressed children were so afraid of undermining students' self-esteem that they failed to criticize conduct or to correct errors adequately. The unfortunate, although predictable, effect was that large numbers of children and their parents were deeply misled about their levels of achievement. Families thus deceived were victims, not beneficiaries.

A third objection has been that the very concept of standards in education is necessarily so utterly subjective and relative as to be incoherent and unusable, and attempts to secure greater objectivity are merely exercises in arbitrariness. Examiners and assessors developed doubts and anxieties, some well justified, about earlier orthodoxies, such as forms of behaviourism which limited objectives to measurable learner behaviour changes. A voluminous literature soon appeared on hard and soft, norm-or criterion-referenced, formative or summative, pre-specified or open-ended modes of evaluation. Genuine objections to inappropriate forms of assessment were often, however, merely a cloak for root-and-branch resistance to every possible mode of assessment. If a wide range of the curriculum is assessed formally, there are complaints of unsupportable burdens on teachers; if only a narrow range is assessed, this is attacked as a narrow preoccupation with the 3Rs and a contempt for vital areas left unassessed, since, it is alleged, some teachers will give serious attention only to the examined elements. No area between the too narrow and too wide is allowable.

Perhaps the most important objection to educational assessment has been the very lack of consensus on educational aims which is a fundamental characteristic of open pluralist societies. It is ironic that the argument that the lack of consensus about educational aims should preclude systematic national testing, even of educational activities consensually accepted as worthwhile and even necessary, should be advanced by those who also claim, when it suits them, that there is consensus about educational aims, that they represent it and that they intend to impose a National Curriculum based on it. Lack of educational consensus is actually the greatest single justification for wide parental choice among different types of school.

The very limited data on changes in Australian educational standards during the 1980s suggests that significant increases in real terms in *per capita* expenditure at all levels of education had disappointing results. The Tasmanian Department of Education's commendable annual studies of performance revealed maintenance of standards, but no improvements, as did an investigation by the Australian Council for Educational Research (McGaw *et al*, 1989) into literacy and numeracy in Victoria, which compared 1988 standards with those of 1975 and 1980. 1990 levels in respect of standards of attainment of science in Victoria (Adams, Doig and Rosier, 1991) were very similar to those of 1983. 1983/84 standards in science Australia-wide among 14-year-olds were very similar to those of 1970/71 (Keeves, 1992), but in eight of the ten countries tested standards had markedly improved during those years, so that Australia fell from third place out of ten in 1970/71 to sixth in 1983/84.

Whatever other weaknesses have been displayed in Conservative educational policies in Britain since 1979, there has at least been a genuine attempt to ensure that more ample information about educational standards is more widely available. To be sure Conservative Secretaries of State, whether because of poor advice from the educational bureaucracies or through their own shortcomings, have made very heavy weather of the task of increasing public knowledge of educational achievement, but even if they had been as wise as Solomon and/or the Queen of Sheba, the educational establishment would still have attacked them either for testing too much and thus overburdening the teachers or of testing too little and thus demonstrating their indifference or even contempt for the wider cultural curriculum. Australian governments have hardly embarked on the task of ensuring that accurate knowledge about educational standards, irrespective of level of detail or extent of coverage, is available to the Australian public. In general there seems little difference between Conservative governments in Britain and ALP governments in Australia in enthusiasm for at best inadequate and at worst highly illiberal instrumentalist and vocationalist strategies to combat the follies and excesses of the radical-progressive era.

The New Instrumentalism

As they become more accustomed to power many radicals and progressives in Australian educational bureaucracies favoured a politically-correct national curriculum with sufficient monitoring to enable them to identify ideological defaulters. Such proposals were also intended to deflect growing public disquiet about educational standards. New programs around 1990 which purported to monitor and report levels of student achievement in key areas of the school curriculum included the New South Wales Basic Skills Testing Program, the Victorian Achievement Studies, the Western Australian Monitoring Standards in Education Program, the Queensland Assessment of Student Performance and the South Australian Levels of Attainment and Writing and Reading Assessment Programs. Since these programs were not designed to reveal whether standards were rising, falling or staying put, concern about educational standards continued to increase outside the education industry, among trade union leaders as well as employers, among left-wing as well as right-wing politicians. The 1991 Finn Review of Young People's Participation in Post-compulsory Education gave expression to widespread worries about poor skill levels among school leavers as did the parallel Mayer Review commissioned by the Australian Education

Council and the 1992 Carmichael Report on an Australian Vocational Certificate Training System. These three reports shared a deep distrust for policies pursued by professional educators for the previous twenty years. They also held that a highly vocational thrust to secondary education would provide the necessary corrective, although there are only weak grounds for supposing the weaknesses they identified were the result of too much general and too little vocational education in the secondary schools. A recurrently bizarre feature to campaigns in Europe and North America, as well as Australia, for more vocational education is that they peak at the point in the jobs cycle when there are fewest jobs to be filled.

Secondary education in economically successful Japan is even less vocational than in Britain or Australia. Germany, on the other hand, also economically successful and like Japan seemingly less beset than comparable English-speaking countries by aimless and alienated adolescents and young adults, has a secondary school system which for some two-thirds of students is highly vocational in orientation. In their reactions against radical-progressivist education Conservative governments in Britain and ALP governments in Australia have been more influenced by the German model. Some key contextual differences may make the German example inapplicable, however. The first is that vocational education has become associated in Britain and Australia, and even more in the United States, with failure in more academic courses and with equity provision for disadvantaged groups. Course and certification requirements have often been minimal and a version of Gresham's Law has resulted in low prestige and limited value in the job market. The recent Australian vocational initiatives have tried to avoid this pitfall. The Finn Review, for example, placed great emphasis on 'key areas of competence'. Some of these are identifiable areas of knowledge, such as language and communication, mathematics and scientific and technological understanding. Others are of a more nebular character, including problems solving, creative thinking and personal and interpersonal skills, said to include 'knowledge and skills related to personal management and planning, including career planning, negotiating and team skills, initiative and leadership, adaptability to change, self-esteem, ethics'. The Mayer Committee listed even more hazy 'key competency skills', including 'collecting, analyzing and organizing ideas and information', 'expressing ideas and information', 'planning and organizing activities', 'monitoring one's own performance and ensuring effective communication', 'working with others and in teams', and 'solving problems: identifying and framing the nature of problems and devising suitable strategies of response'. To circumvent the danger that the world of professional educators might entirely frustrate its purposes, the Mayer Committee suggested that its reference points for competency skills should be the Australian Standards Framework developed by the National Training Board's *Policy and Guidelines*. Its four 'levels of performance' are based on industrial classifications for competent operative or service sector workers, advanced operative or service sector workers, competent skilled autonomous workers, and advanced skilled autonomous workers respectively. The Mayer Committee acknowledged that these key competency levels do not relate to a comparable level of performance in all industries. Even less closely do they relate to levels of educational achievement.

Even if, which remains undemonstrated, good vocationally-oriented courses prepare students for a particular job or range of jobs better than do good liberal-general courses, this would not itself justify the Mayer Committee's call for the 'convergence of general and vocational education', let alone a major replacement of general courses by vocational ones. What is surely indisputable is that well-informed people hold very different views on what should be the balance between liberal/general and instrumental/vocational education or on the appropriate way in which a preferred policy should be implemented. There seems no reason why choice and preference should not be extended on the demand side to as many students, parents and employers as possible and on the supply side to the maximum number of potential providers of courses.

Liberal Education and the State

Child-centred educators have usually preferred devolution of educational decision-making, some even to each child or to children as a peer group, but many liberal educators, fearful of the crude instrumentalism often expressed by pupils, parents and employers have favoured State direction, at least if and when people of their own way of thinking influence governments. Leading British thinkers a century ago or so who looked to the State rather than to parents to extend liberal education included T.H. Green, Arthur Acland, Robert Burdon Haldane, Henry Jones, Michael Sadler and Robert Morant, followed in the next generation by R.H. Tawney , Fred Clarke and A.D. Lindsay. Yet, although the Althusserian thesis was ludicrously exaggerated, governments, once possessed of sufficient power, are easily tempted to politicize curricula and to place short-term objectives before longer-term aims. Furthermore, the strong tendency of parents with children in non-Government schools to choose schools more rather than less liberal in curriculum than government schools suggests that liberal educators should follow John Stuart Mill's advice. This issue is entwined with some which arise in transcendental education.

Transcendental Education and the State

In every European state for a millennium from the seventh to the seventeenth centuries uniformity of faith was regarded as a political as well as a religious necessity and established churches took the lead in extirpating heretical teaching. In contrast, over the last two centuries in all liberal-constitutional states there has been increasing separation between church and state. The extent to which non-Government schools, especially those of a religious character, have received funding which gave them something like effective equality of educational opportunity with government schools has varied greatly among liberal-constitutional states. For example, from the 1870s until the 1960s Britain's Australian colonies (subsequently the Australian states) gave no financial aid to non-governmental schools, causing a deep sense of injustice among Australian Roman Catholics in particular, whereas the different systems in the United Kingdom provided relatively generous financial support to non-Government, including Roman Catholic, schools.

For most of the twentieth century government school systems in English-speaking countries accepted, implicitly at least, what Robert Bellah (1975) termed 'civil religion', a series of moral prescriptions and proscriptions based loosely on traditional Judaeo-Christian teaching, but without commitment to any specific religious doctrines. Civil religion in this sense was rejected by the Roman Catholic Church but found satisfactory by most Protestants, including fundamentalists, whose forerunners had indeed often taken the lead in opposing dogmatic teaching in schools, the dogma being that of established churches they considered to be in error. From the 1960s this civil religion was undermined by the antinomianism then advanced by radical-reconstructionists, with the result that larger numbers of Protestant fundamentalists turned away from Government schools. The rapid expansion of Protestant fundamentalist schools seems to have been in origin less a positive evangelical initiative than a defensive reaction to increasingly militant secularism of Government school systems.

Many of their sharpest critics concede that Protestant fundamentalist schools satisfy many instrumentalist as well as transcendentalist criteria. Peshkin (1989) acknowledged that in the United States their students:

> achieve above average scores on national tests, they receive good instruction in English; and they are taught by hardworking, dedicated teachers. Christian schools create a safe environment in physical and moral terms; they emphasise character training; they promote a sense of community; and according to my data, their students are noted for their low alienation and also for personal qualities that make them attractive to local employers. (pp. 48–9)

Peshkin expressed alarm, however, that such students:

> are taught to see the world in the dichotomised terms of us and them, with the clear-cut good guys — the born-again brethren — learning to stay separate on principle from the clear-cut bad guys — the rest of us . . . children readily acquire the terms for stereotyping: secular humanist Satan, and the world, on the one hand, and believer, born-again, and Christian on the other. (*ibid*, p. 51)

Peshkin praised 'the principled protection of aberrant institutions', which, as he rightly says, 'is not commonly found elsewhere in the world' (that is, outside the liberal democracies), but has become 'bred in the bones of our society' and 'integral to the particular form we give pluralism'. Nonetheless he had some sympathy for the case that the American state has a 'compelling interest' requiring it to forbid the indoctrinative practices engaged in by Protestant Fundamentalist schools. More hostile critics than Peshkin hold that there is such a 'compelling interest' and urge governments to regulate and preferably suppress schools with priorities significantly different from their own (*ibid*, p. 52).

This issue is now acute in many liberal constitutional states in respect of non-Christian groups. For Muslims who conform to the *Sunna*, obstacles to achieving their religious aims are even greater than for Christians, not only because they live in countries little influenced by their own traditions but because Islam has remained a total way of life and, unlike many Christian missionaries and nearly all their anthropological successors, seeks to remain aloof from local error or deviation and rejects syncretic compromises. Specific educational demands typically made by Muslims include:

single sex schools after the age of puberty and traditionally appropriate dress for each sex;

distinctive sex roles to be taught in accord with the Koran;

science teaching in accord with the Koran;

prohibition of representational art, especially of the human figure, and of many Western forms of music;

provision of *Halal* food and facilities for ritual absolution.

Compliance with such demands seems very likely to leave Islamic chidren ignorant of much of the cultural life of Western societies to a much greater extent than do distinctive requirements in any Christian or Jewish schools. The full programme of Islam requires the rote learning of the whole Koran by early adolescence and mastery of the classical Arabic in which it is written, not a few periods of teaching about Islam within multifaith social or religious studies syllabuses.

We must anticipate demands by Muslims for freedom to found Islamic schools and for financial and other support from governments on comparable terms to that given to Christian schools. Such demands will be based partly on Islam's claims to truth and partly on pluralist arguments which Muslims would not entertain in Islamic societies. Islam is in principle deeply opposed to the pluralist ideas it sometimes invokes when seeking rights or status within non-Islamic societies. Yet, although it is always right to expose double standards, this exposure does not provide a basis on which to decide which cultural and educational niches Western societies should, in their own interests, afford to Islam, or indeed to Christian fundamentalists. Islamic fundamentalism has a mass appeal and there is a danger of massive alienation from the best Western traditions of large numbers of young people born here, not just of their overseas-born parents. Direct initiation by government schools of Muslim boys and girls into life in a pluralist liberal-democracy may be difficult to achieve, however well it is carried out. Resistance of some Islamic groups to features of our way of life that our schools currently strive to persuade all newcomers to adopt, including equal access of women to public and professional life, is a legitimate concern, but it is very likely that Western culture will exert great influence on Muslim youth, especially perhaps on girls, many of whom may prefer the position of females in our societies to that in traditional Islam. There may be sharp and continuing culture conflicts among

Muslim families, but that is much preferable to the creation or strength-
ening of a unified hostility among Muslims towards the host society.
Exclusion of Muslims from financial support comparable to that of
Christian churches for schools may strengthen feelings of alienation
from our political values. On the other hand a much wider degree of
parental choice in education might help to deepen a genuine attachment to the new society. Provided that success in an efficient public
examination system is the pathway to professional success, there would
be considerable parental resistance in Islamic schools, as there is now
in Christian schools, against extreme cultural compartmentalization and
anti-intellectual tendencies.

Conclusion

I have not discussed here vouchers and other methods by which families might be empowered to exert much greater educational choice, but
such systems are certainly workable (West, 1982; Peacock, 1983; Seldon,
1986). It is not their feasibility but their desirability which is the key
issue. Many educationists who proclaim a deep concern for the interests of the working class and other disadvantaged groups, and who
profess great admiration for their culture, express alarm at the prospect
that the poorer might be enabled to exert much more extensive educational choice, more akin to that currently available only to the richer
in our society. Some of the very people who block public access to
adequate information about educational standards explain regretfully
that many people are too ignorant to make properly informed judg-
ments about what education is suitable for their children. The greatest
elitism and intellectual pride is displayed by those whose stock-in-trade
includes ritual denunciations of elitism.

During the nineteenth century a common radical objection to non-
Government schooling was that institutions of the 'dame school' type
gave an inferior education. Today the complaint is more often that non-
Government schools are superior and so give an unfair advantage to
those who attend them, although other radicals hold that only snobs
and reactionaries consider non-Government schools better and that, all
background factors allowed for, Government schools are just as good
as them. Some who object to choice in education claim that it leads to
greater inequalities than does the imposition of uniformity, yet disparities in educational achievement between government schools in the
most and least affluent areas are far greater than the mean difference
between government and non-Government schools. It seems highly

inequitable to permit alternatives to the rich whilst denying them to the poor.

Diversity may be extended within government systems through decentralization, school autonomy and local choice, but, as currently in England and Ontario, governments which claim to give wide powers of discretion to individual schools actually retain substantial central control over them . . . When, in New Zealand, many local bureaucracies replace one large central one, the problems posed by cultural diversity and educational contestability are not necessarily overcome and may not even be reduced: minorities forced to accept educational policies they detest may well dislike the tyranny of the parish pump as much as that of central bureaucracy. To ensure significantly wider freedom of parental choice strong local autonomy would have to be backed by open enrolment and encouragement to principals and teachers to develop schools of genuinely distinctive characters.

A person wishing to buy a car may prefer speed to comfort, economy to reliability, and so on. Education is more important than transport and educational policies and decisions are more difficult to make than those about what car to buy. All car buyers expect reliable and accurate information about all these aspects of vehicles among which they will choose and *a fortiori* parents, who also have differing priorities, are entitled to know not only what are the aims and objectives of a particular school but the extent to which these are being achieved. If governments did properly in education what they seem to do fairly adequately in vehicle manufacture and advertising, such as establish and implement safety standards and require that extensive and reliable information about performance and fuel consumption as well as safety is fully available to all interested parties, the situation would be better than it is.

In Australia, Britain and most other liberal-democratic societies we have been too close to the worst of both worlds: educational monopoly without adequate monitoring and public information about standards of achievement. Far better to seek competition combined with adequate monitoring and public information. If proper encouragement were given to individuals and groups to articulate their educational aims and priorities, if financial policies converted these wants into effective demand, and if those with initiative were free to try to meet that demand, the role of the state in education could be greatly diminished and the successful involvement of the population at large in educational decisions be greatly enhanced. Indeed instrumentalist aims of governments, whether relating to vocational skills or work habits and moral formation and irrespective of whether they are adequate aims, are likely to be more fully and more cheaply achieved by educational institutions outside the direct control of governments than by direct Government provision.

The depth and range of educational contestability ensures that educational policies determined by national or state governments are vulnerable to sudden and destructive changes. Nearly every English educational institution in which I was a pupil or teacher underwent massive transformation between 1961 and 1976 at the hands of Labour central governments or local authorities. Many of these have had nearly as turbulent a time under Conservative control since 1979. Incessant governmentally-imposed institutional reorganization has beset my field of work in South Australia since I came here in 1976 and scarcely a single change has been claimed subsequently as a success, even by its most enthusiastic supporters in terms of their own values and priorities. Devolution of decision-making to parents and individual institutions, although sometimes denounced as opening floodgates to unpredictability, is more likely to bring about gradual and piecemeal responses to new problems and to enable the experience of the many to contribute as fully as possible to the educational development of the state. As Mill understood, the logical consequence of contestability in a pluralist society is the abandonment of the search for educational uniformity.

References

ADAMS, R.J., DOIG, B.A. and ROSIER, M. (1991) *Science Learning in Victorian Schools: 1990*, Hawthorn, Victoria, Australian Council for Educational Research.

AUSTRALIAN EDUCATION COUNCIL (1991) Young People's Participation in Post-Compulsory Education and Training: Report of the Australian Education Council Review Committee (Finn Report), Canberra, Australian Government Printing Service.

AUSTRALIAN EDUCATION COUNCIL AND MINISTERS OF VOCATIONAL EDUCATION, EMPLOYMENT AND TRAINING (1992) Putting General Education to Work: The Key Competencies Report (Mayer Report), Canberra, Australian Government Printing Service.

BECKER, G. (1962) *Human Capital*, New York, National Bureau of Economic Research.

BELLAH, R.N. (1975) *The Broken Contract: American Civil Religion in a Time of Trial*, New York, Seabury Press.

BRANSON, J. and MILLER, D. (1979) *Class, Sex and Education in Capitalist Society*, Malvern, Victoria, Sorrett Publishing.

COMMISSION ON THE SKILLS OF THE AMERICAN WORKFORCE (1990) The Australian Vocational Certificate Training Systems (Carmichael Report), Canberra, Australian Government Printing Service.

EMPLOYMENT AND SKILLS FORMATION COUNCIL (1992) The Australian Vocational Certificate Training System (Carmichael Report), Canberra, Australian Government Printing Service.

GALLIE, W.B. (1968) *Philosophy and the Human Understanding*, New York, Schocken Books.

HARRIS, K. (1988) 'The politics of educational research: From a philosopher's point of view', *Educational Research and Perspectives*.

HOLMES, M. (1992) *Educational Policy for the Pluralist Democracy: The Common School, Choice and Diversity*, London, Falmer Press.

KEEVES, J.P. and BOURKE, S.F. (1976) *Australian Studies in School Performance Vol. 2: Literacy and Numeracy in Australian Schools*, Canberra, AGPS.

KEEVES, J.P. (1992) *Learning Science in a Changing World: Cross-national Studies of Science Achievement: 1970 to 1984*, The Hague, International Association for the Evaluation of Educational Achievement.

MAGAW, B., LONG, M.G. and ROSIER, M. (1989) *Literacy and Numeracy in Victorian Schools, 1988*, Hawthorn, Victoria, Australian Council for Educational Research.

MAGLEN, L., MCKENZIE, BURKE, G. and McGAW, B. (1994) 'Investment in Education and Training'. A paper prepared for the Business Council of Australia Summit *Investing in Australia's Future*, Sydney, Melbourne, Australian Council for Educational Research/Centre for the Economics of Education, Monash University, March.

MILL, J.S. (1910) *Utilitarianism, Liberty and Representative Government*, London, Dent and Dutton (Everyman edition).

PEACOCK, A.T. (1983) 'Education voucher schemes — Strong or weak?', in *Economic Affairs*, 3, 2.

PESHKIN, A. (1989) 'Fundamentalist Christian schools: Should they be regulated?', in *Educational Policy*, 3, 1, pp. 45–56.

SCHULTZ, T.W. (1961) 'Education and economic growth' HENRY N.B. (Ed) *Social Forces Influencing American Education*, Chicago, IL, University of Chicago Press.

SELDON, A. (1986) *The Riddle of the Voucher: An Inquiry into the Obstacles to Introducing Choice and Competition in State Schools*, London, Institute of Economic Affairs.

WEST, E.G. (1982) 'Economic vouchers: Evolution or revolution?', in *Economic Affairs*, 3, 1.

4 Schooling and the State: A Review of Current Issues

Beatrice Avalos-Bevan

Introduction

The intention of this chapter is to highlight and discuss questions and assertions relating to schooling, from the perspectives of the State's (also understood as states or provinces where decentralization prevails) involvement in conducting policy discussions and in shaping policies, as well as of its role in furthering changes within the school system. Given my recent experience of a major project to revamp the secondary system in Chile, I will tend not only to focus the chapter particularly on secondary education, but also to scatter it with examples from the Chilean scene.

A quick review of recent literature on policy issues across different country situations, which also include industrialized contexts such as the United Kingdom and the United States, shows an interesting similarity in the manner of posing the issues, in the policy alternatives being suggested and the role that the State wishes to retain for itself in implementing such alternatives. For example, a recent offer made by the Chilean government to a pay rise request by the teachers (which led to a one-day strike), rather than grant the increase requested was to propose an 'excellency fund' to reward effective teachers. Equally, we read in the *Times Educational Supplement* (17 September 1993) that the British Government is proposing to link teacher salary increases with improved individual teacher performance, a move that is strongly resisted not only by the teachers but also by the schools that are to pilot the scheme.

In the face of limited resources available to ministries of education around the world, we hear similar questions about the extent to which the private sector of the economy may contribute to finance education, seeing that it benefits from the system's graduates, or about training teachers in a more cost-effective way with shorter pre-service education and greater emphasis on apprenticeship schemes within schools, or about how in terms of structure and curricular content the system should respond to the needs of the labour market and who should control this response in an era of tremendous technological development.

The commonality of issues across country contexts would seem to be related to four main factors: (i) similar state concerns about issues as disparate as modernization and cultural relevance, about the reality of financial constraints and about the need for economic growth that does not sacrifice equity; (ii) pointedness of the advice received from aid agencies and in particular from such an important fund lender as is the World Bank[1]; (iii) across-country exchanges through top-level policy maker meetings; and (iv) availability of research and policy documentation that reflects world-wide trends. The precise manner in which such issues are actually embodied in policy statements and reform proposals differs of course from country to country; and it is always of interest to examine the extent to which such proposals relate to the social and economic models which are now so powerfully universalized.

Without attempting to pursue a thorough examination of the degree of penetration of externally induced models in the school policies of developing countries, this chapter endeavours to highlight issues of common discussion as evident from literature and experience. Specifically, attention will be directed first to general policy orientations and then specifically to the curriculum, teachers, school control and diversified secondary education.

Policy Orientations

There is a number of ways of categorizing public policy statements related to schooling and one of them is to use the 'catch' words aimed at convincing others about proposed programmes or directions for change. With that criterion, we note the frequency with which policy orientations are expressed as being 'equity', 'relevance' and 'productivity' oriented.

Equity

This concept has a number of concrete references, but in its broadest sense it embodies the concept of 'education for all' so aptly articulated in the Jomtien Declaration as a programme for all countries, but especially for the most poor. While the concept of equity can be interpreted as quantitative educational opportunities for all regardless of social origin, race, ability or gender, it also means quality education for all, and in this meaning it is very much at the centre stage of policy discussions today. More and more it is recognized that the benefits of schooling both to the individual and to a country's development are not just related to the fact of having spent some years in school; but to the completion of a school cycle that has equipped the person not only with communication and numeracy skills but with cognitive abilities of a higher order and with practical competencies to deal with the environment. And this is an issue of quality, which countries view in different ways, along with their concerns about equity. The chances offered to ethnic groups located at the lower levels of the social system concern societies with high levels of ethnic inequality such as the United States[2] while the broader issue of equal opportunities for women is particularly strong in countries where the status of women has been markedly different from that of men.

Relevance

This is a concept fraught with more ambiguity than is the case with equity. In the most straightforward education policy declarations it is simply presented as the capacity of response to the needs of individuals and of the nation-state as a whole. From the perspective of individuals, it is often articulated as education which accords with the wishes of parents or the needs of diverse ethnic and linguistic communities. But relevance as interpreted by parents may not have the same meaning as what the State considers to be its requirements for economic development or national unity. In a country such as Papua New Guinea, where the word 'relevance' has high status in policy declarations, a multiplicity of interpretations flow from different sectors seeing it either as education that serves the rural sector where most of the population lives, or that reaffirms the cultural diversity of the people, or that is responsive to the need to develop a modern economy handled by competent nationals. In Latin America, relevance has also connotations of appropriateness to handle cultural diversity but, more strongly now, it is interpreted in its links to economic growth, modernization and technological improvement. Whichever way the rationale for relevance is presented, the underlying important factors are the political and social agendas of governments, which in the case of secondary education often means preparing 'youth to fill wage-sector jobs, to raise the proficiencies of aspiring university entrants' and 'to reinforce nation-building' (Fuller and Holsinger, 1992).

Productivity

The investment governments make in education, whatever its level, requires some concern for effectiveness and tangible results. More and more the concept of results, as expressed in policy documents, indicates preoccupation about productivity levels related to student achievement, to the social well-being and value-driven conduct of citizens (less youth crime or drug problems), as well as to higher levels of employment and national income. Information on achievement is elicited through systems of national or other examinations. Governments seek information also in one way or another (often public opinion) on the non-cognitive outcomes of the system; and on the destination of secondary school graduates which also concerns the aid agencies.[3] More and more information is being produced or requested on the relationship between GDP levels of countries and expansion of their educational systems. Fuller and Holsinger (*ibid*) report, for example, on a recent World Bank study that found secondary education enrolments in many developing countries (with the exception of South Asia) being positively related to GDP levels over the past three decades; while other studies with similar results were noted by Benavot (1992). Obviously decisions to expand or contract the system of education may be forcefully influenced by the availability of such information.

Schooling Issues

There are numerous issues that are at the centre of attention of policy discussion around the world, but some of them clearly stand out not only as important but as indicative of the concerns for equity, relevance and productivity noted above. These refer to questions about the curriculum, about teachers, ownership and management of schools and about the proper location of preparation for work (technical-vocational education). I shall deal with these below.

The Curriculum

The broad issues regarding the curriculum that have occupied discussions in the last five to eight years refer either to what, in terms of content, people need to know for a variety of purposes, or to what sort of value system and vision of society is being communicated through the curriculum. This in turn has led to the taking of positions regarding who develops and controls the implementation of the curriculum, what kind of curriculum is needed for nation-development or economic growth, and how to measure its productivity.

Role of the State in Shaping the Curriculum

In theory it is possible to see a continuum going from strong State control in the development and management of the curriculum to strong local and teacher control (decentralized systems) such as existed in the United Kingdom until the recent educational reform. In practice, from the perspective of developing country situations, curricular decentralization has rarely been fully implemented on the basis that teachers lack experience and expertise to work from broad curricular guidelines to specific classroom curricular contents. It has been considered safer to provide teachers with detailed content, activities and assessment specifications, and to do so from the centre of the system (curriculum units at Ministry of Education level) through appropriate legislation. On the other hand, industrialized countries like the United Kingdom, Australia, Canada or the United States have had a converse experience: the structure of the curriculum has been broadly specified from the centre, be it the national or state governments, and practically developed and implemented at classroom level with the support of technical organizations such as was the Schools' Council in Britain.

Judging from what is happening in some countries with a traditionally decentralized curriculum, we might speak of a move in the eighties to tighten the control of the State over the curriculum, a move that is rationalized on the basis of the need to 'return to basics' and 'improve standards'. Such is the case of Britain's educational reform or for that matter, within the limitations of the federal structure, of the 'first wave' reforms in the United States calling for a centralization of curriculum shaping and the establishment of a core curriculum with assessable attainment targets indicating the system's productivity.

There is a number of interpretations regarding this tightening of the control of the State over the curriculum occurring at the time when a market economy with a weakened role for the State is so strongly on the upsurge; one of these refers to political agendas and political forces as upholders of change or upholders of traditions and the powerful role of the curriculum itself. Jansen (1991) citing various authors refers to the curriculum as a 'site of contestation because it embodies the values, norms, objectives, interests, priorities, and directions of the State and other powerful sectors of society'. Others in fact describe the implemented curriculum as a set of transactions between political and other social forces (MECE Media, Project 1.1, 1993). In societies such as Zimbabwe, Jansen argues, the State as principal custodian of nation-building is entrusted with determining the curriculum most apt for this purpose. What it does to implement a curriculum in accordance with the political orientation of that society (with an agenda of transition to socialism), is limited in practice by powerful constraints (inherited from the past, or present in the structure of the society itself); affecting in turn the conditions for curricular change. Jansen judges that the curriculum in Zimbabwe has not changed in the direction desired by the political power because of the strength of other social forces, and also because of the impact of the new wave of curriculum issues expressed in non-socialist terms as 'increasing efficiency, raising standards, and improving quality'.

This 'political-power' interpretation regarding the issue of curricular control merits some further exploration for which it may be illustrative to take the case of Britain and of Chile as two sites of recent changes in curricular policy running in different directions. In fact while the educational changes in the United Kingdom and Chile respond to the same logic of making the system of education responsive to the needs of the economy, industry and commerce, thus supporting a modern and market-oriented competitive economy, the role given to the State in relation to the curriculum is different in both contexts. In one case, the State assumes greater control over the shaping in detail of a core curriculum while in the other, the State is relieved of its former obligation to shape the details of the curriculum.

One way of explaining what we might call a strategic difference, is to posit that the goal in both cases is not primarily what it appears to be, that is, it is not primarily a goal linked to a modernizing interest, but rather a goal derived from political agendas, and implemented because there is political power or because political power is in danger of being lost. A view among those who analyze the curriculum reform in Britain is that the push for centralization and control was more than an effort to adapt or meet 'the demands of economic, scientific and technological change and was really the result of an effort to respond to traditional issues of national control and reproduction of the existing social order' (Simon, 1992, p. 140). Goodson (1990) suggests further that the balance of subjects in the National Curriculum reinforces a type of society supportive of the traditions of one part of the country against the other, traditions which are embodied in the political agenda of the party that carries out the reform.

The situation in Chile is different. From a past history in which the State was mainly responsible for educational provision and where education was described in the 1925 Constitution as having the 'prefer-ential attention of the State', the new Organic Law for Education (1989) defined the role of the State as largely a subsidiary one, and opened the education system to competitive bids in the market square.[4] This law passed just before the end of the military government, was a last minute attempt to ensure that the State would not have the power to use the educational system and its curriculum to develop contents and support values running contrary to the prevailing economic model and the type of society built over the long years of dictatorship. In the Organic Law the role of the State is defined as providing a curricular frame in the form of 'basic objectives and minimum contents' for the system. The specification of contents and implementation strategies, while subject to some central technical support, is left to teachers and schools; this enables schools to request approval of special curricular programmes responding to diverse interests of the schools and parents such as fur-thering the learning of a foreign language and culture or opening the school to more vocational subjects.

Thus, while in Chile curriculum decentralization is justified as in Britain in terms of relevance to the needs of a modern society and to a market economy, the underlying rationale for limiting the role of the State in shaping the curriculum is the need to restrict the power of a new Government to establish a curriculum with contents and values that might run counter to the social and economic model implanted through eighteen years of authoritarian dictatorship.

Economic Growth and the Curriculum

Granted that there is a strong view that the kind of curriculum content adopted in a society will be more or less instrumental in the acquiring of knowledge, skills and attitudes able to further economic growth, a fair amount of curricular discussions centre around what these contents should be.

In agriculture and largely subsistence economies such as Papua New Guinea and many African countries, the discussions on the pri-mary level of education revolve around having a curriculum which provides literacy and numeracy skills preferably in the mother tongue, as well as skills for early participation in the rural economy. The policy concept prevailing in this view is that of relevance, while the concepts of equity and quality are seen as only of secondary importance. There are dissenting views about this. Formulating a critique of the current reform proposals for the curriculum of primary schools in Papua New Guinea (reduction of overall school time, of time for mathematics, English and science, and increase in time for vocational activities), O'Donoghue (1993) believes that while there is no guarantee that the changes will result in a better insertion of children in the rural economy, it will deny them the tools which are needed for higher level cognitive development (mathematical and language skills) and deny the country potential resources for a more technically oriented economy (the contribution of science to the curriculum).

A different justification for a 'relevant' curriculum and one closer to equity policies is advocated for the region of Latin America by a recent joint ECLA/UNESCO (1992) report. Among other things the report calls for improvements in the teaching of language, mathematics and science to enable all young people to understand, interpret and use the codes of technological 'modern' society currently restricted to few sectors within each country of the region. The rationale of the report is that poverty and under development in Latin America can only be diminished if societies achieve substantially higher levels of economic growth for which education needs to prepare the young to take an active part. Though relying more strongly on awareness of the technological world and of the paradigmatic changes occurring in the fields of knowledge and communications than other official policy documents had done before, the ECLA/UNESCO report really reaffirms the 'trickle-down' theories of poverty-reduction and the traditional assigned role of education in economic development. Nevertheless, the report's powerful formula of 'growth with equity' is becoming a unifying motto among liberal political groups wishing to infuse new life into the educational systems of Latin America.

The rationale for the educational reforms of the primary and secondary systems in Chile has been largely influenced by the ECLA/UNESCO report and the policies of 'growth and equity' adopted by the Chilean government. These reforms are aimed at making quality education available to all young people, particularly to those who belong to the poorer sectors of the society. From the perspective of curricular improvement, however, the restricted powers of the State (explained above) make it difficult for the central Government to achieve much more (besides the national framework) than the offering of curricular guidelines, the financing of curricular support materials for teachers, and the support for in-service experiences to improve the quality of educational delivery in schools and processes of teacher-driven curriculum development.

Whether economic growth is better achieved by some curricular subjects as opposed to others is very much a subject of discussion and one about which there is not much research. Vocationalizing a common curriculum is one of the ways in which it is considered that young people can be prepared not only for work in a specific manner but also to understand and value a traditional rural economy or a modern technical society. That was of course John Dewey's view at the turn of the century as he considered the growth of cities and the effects of the Industrial Revolution. Another perspective is to view particular subjects and the way in which they are taught as key ingredients of a modern attitude, the development of modern skills and the preparation for the high quality work aimed at economic productivity and competitiveness. As happened in the past, so also today it is believed that certain abilities such as scientific reasoning, mathematical skills and specific technical skills are better suited to economic development than are the arts and the humanities. There is not much evidence of how true this is, other than a suggestion that a difference in the length of exposure to 'hard subjects' such as maths and science among student populations in Japan and the United States may have affected the differential behaviour of the two countries' economies (Benavot, 1992). One attempt to examine across nations the effect of subject time allocation is reported by Benavot (*ibid*). Using a cross-national and longitudinal research design Benavot examined variations in annual instructional time at the primary level in mathematics, science and six other subject areas within the 1960 to 1985 period and linked these results to changes in GDP over the same time, in sixty nations of which forty-three were less developed countries. The measures of instructional time consisted of the number of school periods or 'school hours' per subject per week and the estimated allocated time in terms of yearly hours. The results of the study (which used a multiple regression methodology with panel data) showed a positive economic impact of total yearly hours of instruction across all subjects; with two subjects having significant effects on economic growth: science with a positive effect and pre-vocational or practical education, a negative effect. Contrary to popular wisdom, no effect was noted of instructional time allocated to maths and language on economic growth. In the case of the less developed nations, Benavot's finding indicated, however, a positive impact of instructional hours devoted to the arts and music. Though these findings are interesting in the light of attempts to reduce curriculum hours to allow for vocational subjects (such as the case of Papua New Guinea referred to above) or to push for emphasis on 'basic skills' in maths and language. Benavot himself warns against them being taken at face value, as there may be alternative explanations for these results which would require exploring.

The apparently positive effect of science time allocation on economic growth as indicated by Benavot's study and the theory of its importance in general for development, may well be considered by those driven also by relevance policies to consider a greater effort to improve science instruction at all levels of the educational system. In fact, Fuller and Holsinger (1992) suggest that science curricula serve important functions which are at the heart of those who search for relevant education: provision of an empirical approach to the solution of problems, acquaintance with innovations associated with agricultural and rural development, sensitizing to problems in the natural environment and introduction to innovations related to health, nutrition and family planning.

Assessment and the Curriculum

In the struggle both for control over curricular contents and for indications about its productivity, countries develop a strong concern about assessment procedures, with the trend being stronger still towards centralized assessment. In general, where the State reserves for itself the right to set the core curriculum and attainment levels, as in the case of the United Kingdom, it may seem a logical consequence that determination of the assessment procedures and tests be also a central concern. In locations, such as Chile, where the State has been left with a weak role in relation to curriculum matters, the control over assessment may appear as a contradictory policy[5]. Yet here also the recent push on the side of those responsible for improving the quality of both primary and secondary education has been to establish a system of cognitive testing to provide indications of attainment in mathematics, language, science and social sciences (core subjects in the curriculum). While this is in place for the primary level it has only been tried experimentally for the secondary level; but there are indications that for this level a much stricter system of national examinations would be considered desirable such as is being implemented in England and Wales or in Scotland.

As we know almost all the Commonwealth countries have national examinations in one form or another, and the struggle to replace the external ones with nationally constructed systems has not been an easy process. According to Fuller and Holsinger (*ibid*), preoccupation about equity and quality are motivating national governments to deal with problems related to the low-level of cognitive skills that are measured, the presence of cultural biases towards or against certain groups in the society and the imbalance between urban/rural-oriented contents. But the value of examinations as measures not so much of productivity of schools as individual entities but of the curriculum and of general levels of attainment over time may not be possible if examinations are written anew every year with different criteria in mind (*ibid*).

Teachers

To a certain extent in many countries there are a number of contradictions related to what is expected of teachers and the way in which the administration of the educational systems regard them in practice. There is, for example, a contradiction between the degree of professional behaviour expected of teachers, especially in the current wave of concerns about quality, and the degree to which teachers are subjected to various forms of control over their decision-making and actions. In other words, teachers are asked to perform competently and to produce good student results while at the same time they are allowed little professional judgment about how and what will enhance these results. Another form of this contradiction, motivated by financial constraints, is the low wage structure especially for primary teachers which does not accord with the roles and responsibilities that teachers must exercise in relation to student learning and to their moral and social behaviour. Having said this in general terms, it may be of use to illustrate these contradictions as they appear in the concrete setting of a decentralized system in which the central authority nevertheless retains strong control over training (of primary teachers), appointments, placements and promotions, inspects teaching and provides in-service opportunities such as is Papua New Guinea; and in a decentralized system where the State has no control over teacher training, appointments and placement but controls in-service opportunities through monetary subsidies to teachers and controls the quality of teaching through supervisory mechanisms, such as is Chile.

Primary teachers in Papua New Guinea are expected to fulfil a role of great responsibility in that they not only must teach children to master the basic skills of literacy and numeracy and learn about contents of a fairly broad curriculum involving science, social science, arts, vocational subjects etc, but also contribute to the development of the communities where their schools are located. In practice, many of the teachers work in isolated localities and because of this experience have little support in their daily tasks. They are all entitled to housing but houses are not always available nor properly equipped or maintained. Teachers are regularly inspected meaning, in most cases, that a check is made as to whether they comply with prescribed teaching structures or formats or whether forms of unacceptable personal behaviour are noticed. On the basis of these inspections teachers may be granted the opportunity to upgrade themselves through in-service opportunities (a good number may be eligible to complete a degree at the University of Papua New Guinea). Teachers in Papua New Guinea are encouraged to make adaptations of the National Curriculum to local conditions and needs; few of them do so, however, because much of the training and teaching advice they receive is geared to following prescribed structures which have been centrally determined. In practice, teachers do not have much of a say in proposals for change although there will always be one or two of them in provincial or national task-forces engaged in reform proposals. Teacher training conditions and approaches are heavily directed from the central offices of the National Department of Education, though there is a strongly contested move to break away from this control through the establishment of a National Institute of Teacher Education as an autonomous body[6]. There is not yet much evidence of influence in Papua New Guinea of a market-type of educational philosophy and the state is still very much the entity responsible for the education of most Papua New Guinea citizens. But it exercises this responsibility still influenced by the patterns of colonial education inherited from the Australian administration, with an embedded mistrust in the capacity of teachers to perform effectively, without specific guidance and surveillance.

The situation in Chile is a different one. To take the example of secondary teachers, they are all trained independently from the State in State-funded or private universities on a four-year programme and the exercise of the profession is not accredited by the State. Most secondary teachers work in urban conditions and most of them in municipal, private, subsidized and corporate technical schools funded by the State; while a minority will work in private non-subsidized schools. Teachers who are paid with State funds earn meagre salaries[7] that are very different from those earned by teachers in the private system. Teachers of municipal schools are appointed and removed by the municipal authority, and there is no real promotion scheme other than moving from teacher status to administrator status. In most schools, except those privately owned or managed by religious communities, teachers have little to say about the running of the school; there are few regular meetings dealing with scholastic issues; equally, teachers are rarely considered as interlocutors in public debates on education, whether conducted or not by the State. Professional support and advice should be found in the first instance in the schools themselves through the Technical Pedagogical Unit; but this in practice is not the case, as most of the advice given relates to the fulfilment of bureaucratic requirements that are issued from the central authorities. Supervisory visits often consist of checks on whether administrative norms are being fulfilled to the extent that the role of supervisors has been described by teachers as that of a 'transmitting belt' from central authorities to the school (MECE, Project 4.2., 1993). Teachers in Chile are caught between the requirements of what is left of ministerial authority as expressed in legislation and norms that require more or less rigid observation, and a decentralized administrative system that more often than not, acts arbitrarily in what it requires schools and teachers to do.

Teaching Performance and Teacher Incentives

One of the ways in which educational systems are beginning to think more pointedly that they can affect the quality of teaching in schools is through provision of incentives, both of monetary and non-monetary types[8].

Incentives of one kind or another have always existed in educational systems such as, for example, rewarding teachers through opportunities of in-service training, or through postings in better situations, or through different types of promotion schemes. But, in the face of increasing financial constraints in the systems and low salary structures there is an increasing pressure to link monetary rewards of one type or another to performance in the classroom and to student results. It is interesting to note that one such scheme was developed in Britain towards the end of the nineteenth century. In fact as recalled by Goodson (1990), the 'Payment by Results' scheme consisted in having teachers' pay linked to pupils' results in school examinations. This was done by setting aside a considerable amount of the grant paid to schools (which included payment of salaries) to be decided on the merits of the schools' results. The effects of the system on teachers was described by a school inspector at the time (Holmes, in Goodson, 1990) as putting incredible pressure on the teachers to conform to the prescriptions of the syllabus and to get the pupils 'through the yearly examination by hook or by crook'.

No such crude form of teacher reward is being proposed at present but there is a dangerous proximity between the concept of 'payment by results' and the approach some governments are using in trying to settle pay claims by teachers, as suggested in the cases of Britain and in Chile referred to earlier in this chapter.

In view of these trends, one may ask if there is evidence of improved teacher performance as a result of incentive schemes? Chapman, Snyder and Burchfield (1993) examined the effect of a number of teacher incentives on teacher career satisfaction and on classroom practice in Botswana. The incentive categories considered included: teacher re-muneration (salary and fringe benefits), availability of instructional materials, instructional supervision, amount of teacher training, oppor-tunities for career advancement and community support and recog-nition. Through observing over 500 teachers' classroom performance and through obtaining their ratings of satisfaction with teaching as a career, the researchers were able to establish the relationships between the quantity and quality of incentives received with these dependent vari-ables. Results (of matching 305 teacher questionnaires with their obser-vation data) indicated in the first place a sameness of teaching practices (extremely teacher-centred classrooms) among most of the teachers that did not allow for any effect of incentives over these practices to be determined. On the other hand, it was possible to establish a number of significant relationships between teacher career satisfaction and mostly non-monetary incentives, such as instructional supervision through more headteacher visits to their classrooms, and guidelines for evaluating pupil performance, community support, in-service training and belief in opportunities for career advancement. The common factor in all these incentives was their interpersonal quality which seems consistent with findings from other research (*ibid*).

What emerges as important from the above study which relates, of course, only to the situation in one country, is that the improvement of teacher classroom performance is not necessarily linked to the provi-sion of incentives and that although career satisfaction may be a factor that creates motivation for improvement of practices, this is not neces-sarily enhanced by impersonal forms of incentives. It is even more important that centrally organized schemes of incentives or the con-verse, which is centrally structured forms of requiring accountability related to classroom performance, may not have the effects desired. The role of the State in improving teaching performance through cen-trally structured forms of incentives or requirements is at the very least, a questionable strategy.

School Control and Management: Private vs. Public

As in the case of the curriculum, we note in relation to school owner-ship and management a continuum between centralized and decentral-ized forms and between State-owned, State subsidized and private schemes. Among the questions arising from change trends in the state control of schools is the rationale for such trends. In their issues paper on secondary education, Fuller and Holsinger (1992) say that:

Rising disaffection with uniform and homogenous secondary schools has sparked interest in more innovative, less secular forms of schooling. Budget constraints facing many central governments have further kindled this interest. The current debate focuses on whether private or single-sex schools (Government or private) are more effective in boosting student achievement overall, or for certain groups (working class or female pupils).

What is curious about this statement, given that in the past and in most countries working-class young people had limited access to private education, is that private education is considered as possibly better able to boost working-class student achievement. In the face of governments' financial inability to deal with deteriorating conditions in State-owned schools, the statement in fact hints at a possible increase in the number of privately owned but perhaps subsidized schools serving poorer student populations, or a voucher system that would allow parents to choose for their children the schools they prefer. To justify such changes evidence is needed on how effective private schools are in boosting the achievement of poorer students.

The trend to privatizing schools is consistent with the market-oriented philosophy that in the best of cases supports parents' rights to choose the kind of school to which they would wish to send their children, and in the worst of cases, in private schools ruled by profit-making motives as opposed to pedagogical goals, discriminates against sectors of the population forced to attend such schools. Decentralized ownership and control of schools, together with support of private schools, became a conscious policy of the Chilean military government throughout the decade of the eighties. This has meant in practice that at present the central authority (the Ministry of Education) does not own any schools. Instead four types of schools have appeared which differ in quality and the opportunities available to students that attend them. These are: schools owned by municipalities, technical schools owned by private industrial corporations, and two other kinds of private schools which either receive grants to support low income students or are entirely dependent on their student fees. Recent research in Chile[9] has shown the extent to which this system of school ownership is not only socially divisive (the poorer sectors have no choice but to attend municipal or corporation schools), but also the extent to which there are complicated and unsatisfactory forms of management as a result of these changes in school ownership. Municipal, corporation and subsidized private schools are all under dual types of control involving the dependency of their institution on the ministry of education which has linked the award of grants to monthly averaging of the number of students attending the school. The municipal schools are really the only inheritors of the old state system, and the former quality of many has swiftly eroded so that at present their student results are the worst across the country; the quality of private subsidized schools is marginally better; and only the fee paying schools can show higher levels of student success — but only the very few top traditional schools. Working conditions for teachers in municipal and private subsidized schools are linked to the amount of subsidies paid to schools and this in turn is linked to student attendance, so that making sure students are sitting in classrooms every day has become a prime preoccupation of teachers and the accurate recording of attendance is a prime duty of school personnel (MECE, Project 2.1, 1993).

The Chilean case may be an extreme illustration of the ill effects of market economy principle applied to the control and management of an educational system, but should serve as a warning light in the face of advice being given in favour of school privatization. Information about private schools elsewhere is variable and as Fuller and Holsinger (1992) point out, the effectiveness of these schools is very much an area of ignorance. Recent research in the United States attempting to find evidence as to whether student achievement differences between public and private schools are important enough to warrant policy recommendations, indicates that they are not. Witte's (1992) research based on a major study comparing private (mostly Catholic) and public schools (*High School and Beyond*) indicated that despite important differences between types of schools in terms of size of school, socio-economic class of students, school environment such as provision of academic type courses or level of truancy and quality of discipline, differences in achievement levels are not substantial. Sector effects for achievement were statistically significant but the size of the effect was very small after controls were made for prior achievement, student background, tracking and course taking. Similarly, studies conducted in Chile (MECE, Projects 3.1 and 4.1, 1993) that measured achievement in mathematics and Spanish indicated that students in none of the different types of schools, whether private or public, reached satisfactory levels, although private non-subsidized schools had higher average achievement levels. Equally, another study (MECE, Project 2.1, 1993) indicated that schools differed greatly in management and school ethos characteristics with the best schools being the Catholic private ones, regardless of whether they were subsidised or not, and the worst being the municipal and corporation schools; schools, however, did not differ in the quality of teaching practices which were generally described as transmissive teacher-centred ones. This research also supported, both for private and non-private schools, research that has indicated the importance of head teacher leadership style in relation to school quality.

Returning to the question of private versus public schools and the provision of opportunities for free choice, Levin's (1992) introduction to the special issue of the *Economics of Education Review* on market choice issues provides further evidence against the belief that poorer sectors may benefit from systems of free choice using voucher schemes. Research on patterns of choice in Scotland, Levin notes, provides no evidence that parents choose schools because of better examination results, but strong evidence of social stratification resulting from choice. On the suggestion that the voucher scheme enables poor parents to select better schools and thereby indirectly influences competitiveness for improvement in school quality, research in Richmond, California, provides no evidence of improvement in such problems as student absenteeism, dropout rates, achievement scores or school desecration. Levin (1992) therefore concludes that 'whether in Scotland, New York state or Richmond, California (a community with a high concentration of unemployment and poverty), it appears that the poor are least likely to pursue their options'.

Secondary Education and the Place of Technical-Vocational Alternatives

Very much linked to the role of the State in offering secondary education that prepares people not just for higher education but for work, is the question of whether or not to support specific secondary programmes of technical education. A major World Bank policy paper (1991) is recommending, contrary to its policies of over a decade ago, that schools are not the best place to train in vocational skills, and that employers should take on this role. The main arguments against maintaining a diversified system of secondary education relate to the costs and the assumption that the quality of offerings never can keep pace with technological change. The policy document recommends that public investment should go into improving the quality of primary and general secondary education rather than in maintaining or creating programmes of technical secondary education. While there is much sense in suggesting that the development of good quality general education is a condition that will perhaps be more appreciated by employers willing to train their workers in specific skills, there are a number of considerations that force the recommendations to be considered with caution. Lauglo (1991) deals with some of these. Against the view that the best skills' training will be offered in the work place, Lauglo indicates that an alternative view is that employment-based training could be especially limited and narrow to suit changing economies, and could therefore affect the skills that a worker trained in this manner would have for another type of employment. Furthermore, Lauglo criticizes as being an extremely naive perspective the belief in a form of inevitable progress from state to private ownership and management of technical training. While acknowledging that much closer collaboration needs to take place between state-controlled technical training and private industry, he warns against 'romanticizing the capacity and willingness of industry to train'. 'Critical scrutiny of public institutions', he says, 'needs to be matched with similar critique of private and industry-based training'. Another of Lauglo's expressions of caution refers to accepting without further exploration of their meaning, statements made by employers that they are happy with general education only for their trainees. What are these elements of general education that make a school leaver trainable? Skills, attitudes, higher-level cognitive processes?

One of the possible projections of the World Bank's policy document into the shaping of practice is being discussed at present by the Chilean government. In reviewing options for improving the quality of secondary education, there is a strong push to alter the current dual structure of the system with its humanistic-scientific and technical-vocational tracks. An ongoing discussion proposes to progressively develop a general secondary school with a lower (terminal for some) and upper level and a curriculum centred on higher cognitive skills and moral and personality development which could serve either the requirements of higher education or training in the work place. However, research commissioned by the Government has shown that the technical-vocational stream in current secondary education is chosen by the parents of poorer sectors of the population because it offers a greater guarantee of employment. More important still is the evidence provided by such research (MECE, Projects 4.2 and 4.3, 1993) that more secondary school leavers from the technical vocational stream as compared with those from the general education stream, find employment in the formal sector after leaving school and also achieve higher income levels over a period of time. Any changes that involve dismantling the secondary technical-vocational stream may well, at least in the short term, be detrimental to the principles of equity which the Government is trying to uphold.

The Lauglo argument and the experience of Chile suggests that more thinking and certainly more research evidence is needed before decisions are taken to push technical-vocational education not only out of the schools system, but further away from publicly supported education which, as seen above, is still the most important alternative for the poor.

Conclusion

I have a certain reluctance to draw conclusions from the issues raised in this chapter because what is intended is to hold them for discussion, in the hope that the experience and research of others will provide evidence in one direction or another. However, a few points can be made which might be of use.

If we consider policy orientations regarding equity, relevance and productivity, the trends to diminish the financial and other involvement of the state in education in many developing countries may be at least questionable. As far as equity is concerned, there appears to be little evidence that increased participation of the private sector in the ownership and management of schools will increase the chances that the poor will receive education of better quality than they get at present in the state-maintained system. School quality and effectiveness seem more related, when differences for socioeconomic status are controlled, to school ethos characteristics, quality of management and quality of teaching, then to private/public ownership factors. Reforms are needed in the light of equity issues in the manner in which both State or private systems manage their schools and the extent to which they regard their teachers as professionals and treat them accordingly. More specifically, what is needed are more imaginative schemes for improving the quality of state-funded schools which in most locations still cater for the large groups of population who have less resources to invest in schooling.

There is a great danger that with the reign of open-market policies and the stimulus to privately-owned education, the concerns for relevance in the broader sense of the term will be lost. The principles of competitiveness and profit which are at the heart of neo-classic economic policies will not be easily reconciled with upholding cultural diversity within the perspective of national solidarity. For better or for worst, governments have a responsibility beyond the private interests of individual groups, to build national consensus around values which are of importance to all groups in the country; the withering away notion of the state which underlies many of the change policies discussed may not be in the best interests of nation-building and national unity.

Productivity, understood also in the broad sense of school success and contribution of education to economic growth may be enhanced by a strong participation of the private sector in the training of labour resources in countries moving swiftly towards industrialization; it may have little to offer in countries where subsistence agriculture is still the main form of living for most people, where other forms of vocational training are desirable. Nations, the people and not private corporations are best able to judge what is needed and where to obtain adequate provision for these needs.

State control of education, especially when it is arbitrarily centralized and highly bureaucratic, has detrimental effects on education; and in no way, should the words of caution expressed in this chapter indicate an unqualified support for that form of control. But the other extreme of education 'up-for-bids in the market place' poses a serious threat to all three of the main policy targets which are voiced today as desirable. What is needed, I think, is careful consideration of the implications of converting an economic model which may be successful today in some contexts, into the frame for determining the structure, conditions and processes for human development.

Notes

1 Samoff's (1993) analysis of the importance of the World Bank as a development adviser suggests that this is closely linked to it being a very good provider of knowledge about development country contexts (for example, it generates crucial and research-based information in the form of Issues of Reviews papers) and also a good manager of this knowledge through its guidelines for policy change.

2 This concern was part of the rationale for the Carnegie Report's (*A National Prepared*, 1986) call among other things to 'mobilize the nation's resources to prepare minority youngsters for teaching careers'.

3 For example, two of the recent studies commissioned by the Chilean Ministry of Education to provide information about the secondary education system were directed to finding out comparatively the employment patterns and income levels of basic school and secondary (humanistic and technical-vocational) leavers.

4 This was largely expressed in the reform of the ownership and administration of schools that included strong stimulation towards the creation of private schools. In the secondary system privately owned schools including those that receive grants from the State now amount to 61.3 per cent of all schools. Parents, it is assumed, are free to choose where they place their children and would do so presumably on the grounds of school quality and relevance to their needs.

5 There is no tradition in Chile of national examinations. Until 1965 the only content-based national examination was conducted by the University of Chile with the purpose of determining admission to the university system. With the reform of 1965, two different examinations were instituted. A national 8th grade examination (discontinued after 1973) and an aptitude test to establish capabilities for university studies. The Academic Aptitude Test is full of problems regarding what it measures as well as its almost exclusive higher education studies orientation.

6 The establishment of such an Institute, as an autonomous professional body of support to teacher training institutions, was approved by the National Education Board agreeing to the drafting of legislation to be submitted to Parliament; yet, from two different quarters in the Ministry of Education there is a request to reexamine the autonomous character this institution might have, before any submission proceeded to Parliament.

7 The 1992 average yearly salary for a 30-hour contract was $1,403,964 (Chilean pesos) representing around US$3500. Little wonder that teachers work in two or three schools at one time to draw a salary that will allow them to support their families.

8 The Chilean efforts to improve the quality of teacher performance in the classroom include the provision of monetary rewards to 'excellency', as well as other non-monetary incentives such as availability of equipment and teaching resources, support for better supervision of teachers and opportunities to improve their classroom practices through in-school reflective workshops.

9 The Ministry of Education's current programme to improve the quality of secondary education commissioned a set of thirteen pieces of research on the system that have provided up-to-date information on many of the problems besetting the school arrangements inherited from the military Government.

References

BENAVOT, A. (1992) 'Curricular content, educational expansion and economic growth', *Comparative Education Review*, 36, 2, pp. 150–175.

CHAPMAN, D.W., SNYDER JR., C.W. and BURCHFIELD, S.A. (1993) 'Teacher incentives in the third world', *Teachers & Teacher Education*, 9, 3, pp. 301–16.

ECLA/UNESCO (1992) *Education and Knowledge: Basic Pillars of Changing Production Patterns with Social Equity*, Santiago de Chile, UNESCO.

FULLER, B. and HOLSINGER, D.B. (1992) *Secondary Education in Developing Countries. Issues Review. Draft Issues Review Paper*, Washington, DC, World Bank.

GOODSON, I.F. (1990) '"Nations at Risk" and "National Curriculum": Ideology and identity', *Politics of Education Association Yearbook*, pp. 219–32.

JANSEN, J. (1991) 'The state and curriculum in the transition to socialism: The Zimbabwean experience', *Comparative Education Review*, 35, 1, pp. 76–91.

LAUGLO, J. (1992) 'Vocational and technical education and training: A World Bank policy paper, essay review', *Comparative Education Review*, 36, 2, pp. 227–36.

LEVIN, H.M. (1992) 'Market approaches to education: Vouchers and school choice', *Economics of Education Review*, 11, 4, pp. 279–85.

MECE, Project 1.1 (1993) *Description y Evaluacion del Proceso de Desarrollo Curricular*, Santiago de Chile, MINEDUC.

MECE, Project 2.1 (1993) *Practicas de Trabajo y Socializacion en Establecimientos de Ensenanza Media*, Santiago de Chile, MINEDUC.

MECE, Project 3.1 (1993) *Determinacion de la Calidad de la Educacion Chilena*, Santiago de Chile, MINEDUC.

MECE, Project 4.1 (1993) *Indicadores de Cobertura y Calidad de la Educacion Media Chilena*, Santiago de Chile, MINEDUC.

MECE, Project 4.2 (1993) *Destino Educativo Laboral de lost Egresados de la Educacion Media Chilena*, Santiago de Chile, MINEDUC.

MECE, Project 4.3 (1993) *Evaluacion Economica de la Educacion Media en Chile*, Santiago de Chile, MINEDUC.

O'DONOGHUE, T. (1993) 'Community development and the primary school teacher in the developing world: An analysis of recent trends in Papua New Guinea', *Teachers & Teacher Education*, 9, 2, pp. 183–91.

SAMOFF, J. (1993) 'The reconstruction of schooling in Africa', *Comparative Education Review*, 37, 2, pp. 181–222.

SIMON, B. (1992) *What Future for Education?*, London, Lawrence and Wishart.

WITTE, J.F. (1992) 'Private schools versus public school achievement: Are there findings that should affect the educational choice debate?', *Economics of Education Review*, 11, 4, pp. 371–94.

WORLD BANK (1991) *Vocational and Technical Education and Training: A World Bank Policy Paper*, Washington, DC, World Bank.

5   Private Higher Education and External Control

Joseph Stetar

One of the most important issues surrounding the international support and operation of higher education in recent years is the relative merits and strengths of public (State) and private (independent) colleges and universities. Until recent years serious discussions regarding the role of private higher education in national education policy were often characterized as being of idiosyncratic importance to American and Japanese policy analysts. After all, the United States and Japan were the only highly developed countries with any significant private sectors and the Japanese sector woefully underfunded and over enrolled in the 1970s and 1980s sometimes paled in comparison to the vigour of its American brethren.[1]

While American public and private universities and colleges have long existed side by side, as Burton Clark of the University of California at Los Angeles points out, in recent American history there has been a decided shift toward public institutions, with the general prognosis suggesting that private colleges and universities will continue to erode in size and importance. Until recent decades private higher education has tended to dominate America. In 1950/51 there were 1859 institutions of higher education in the United States of which 638 were public and 1221 private. By 1980 the figures had significantly shifted and there were 3270 institutions, 1510 public and 1760 private (Cardozier, 1987, pp. 23–5). Figures provided by the US Department of Education covering the year 1991/92 report there are 1598 public and 1603 private colleges and universities[2]. The relative growth of the two sectors is illustrated below:

Figure 5.1: Institutions of higher education in US

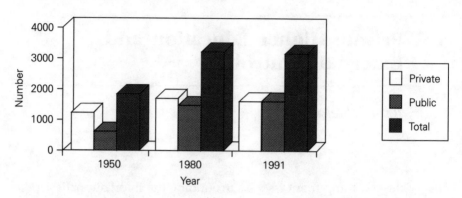

The rapid growth of the public sector in the United States is perhaps even better illustrated by looking at enrolment. While the percentage of students enroling in the private sector declined only marginally in the 1980s there has, as the following chart illustrates, been a significant shift in the proportion of students enrolled in private colleges and universities over the last four decades:[3]

Figure 5.2: Percentage of US students enrolled in private higher education: 1950–1991

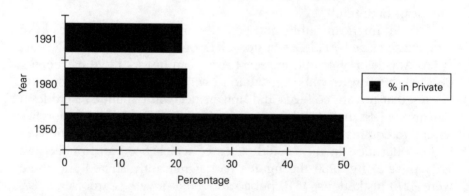

Despite these significant enrolment shifts private institutions, large and small, universities and colleges, continue to have impressive prestige and retain a powerful position in American society. Are these private colleges and universities, as Burton Clark appropriately questions, merely anti-quated, elitist vestiges of an earlier era? Do they duplicate, at greater cost to the taxpayers, the efforts of public institutions? Do they contribute in special ways to the culture, economy and educational life in America or are they merely refuges for the new bourgeois? Is the United States of America's commitment to private higher education an international anomaly or does it have parallels in other nations? Is private higher education a dying concept or does it warrant renewed consideration by academics and public policy makers in both developed and developing nations? Is higher education not a public responsibility — and should the state rather than private groups not therefore provide it?[4] How can we best answer such questions?

While numerous developed societies (for example, much of Western Europe) have seemed to find private higher education unnecessary or in certain instance even inimical it has been embraced in recent decades by many of the least developed nations. However, this infatuation with private higher education is not limited to the Third World. Plans for private colleges and universities are surfacing like wild flowers in several of the former Eastern Bloc countries. In Russia, for example, institutions of higher education such as S M Kirov Textile and Light Industry Institute in St Petersburg[5] and instructional and training units such as the Academy of Pedagogical Sciences in Moscow and The Association of Experts on Professional Training of the Russian Academy of Sciences have plans in various stages of formation for privatization[6]. In Belarus, private higher education is being proffered by business, religious and cultural leaders as a means for accelerating economic growth and fostering cultural and ethnic solidarity while helping to circumscribe state suzerainty. And as developed nations, confronted by the pressures for greater democratization move from elite to mass higher education, the staggering costs associated with such a transition are forcing a fresh consideration of private higher education. There is, therefore, a need for a careful reconsideration, from a cross-cultural perspective, of the potential benefits and liabilities associated with the privatization of higher education.[7]

Attempts to examine private higher education quickly come to the difficulty of defining what is meant by private higher education. In the United States, the distinction between private and public or State higher education has become increasingly blurred in recent decades. Many private colleges now receive substantial assistance from their State governments while public institutions have raised tuitions and have grown aggressive in seeking private funds[8]. The ambiguity regarding public — private institutions is also deeply rooted in the literature. Levy (1986) uses three categories: finance, governance and function in an attempt to arrive at working definitions of private and public higher education:

- **Finance**: an institution is private to the extent it receives its income from non-government sources and public to the extent it relies on the State.

Figure 5.3

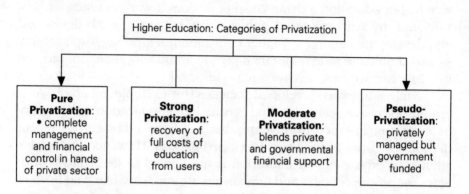

- **Governance**: an institution is private to the extent it is governed by non-State personnel and public to the extent it is governed by the State.
- **Function**: this characteristic is quite vague but in general it seeks to determine the extent to which an institution assumes a public mission and how that relates to governance and finance.

Jandhyala Tilak, a Professor with the Educational and Finance Unit at the National Institute of Education Planning and Administration in New Delhi, contributes to our definitions of private and public by providing four distinct categories for determining privatization (Utley, 1992).

How is Private Higher Education Organized Internationally?

In his important seminal study, *Private Sectors in Higher Education: Structure, Function and Change in Eight Countries*, Roger Geiger (1986) divides private sectors of higher education into three distinct categories: mass, parallel and peripheral.

Mass private sectors such as those in Japan and the Philippines, which enrol 78 and 85 per cent of all university students in those two countries, respectively, flourish in an environment where private colleges complement a public sector limited in size, selective in admission and generally oriented toward the more elite tasks of higher education. Beginning early in the twentieth century as advanced specialized colleges or upgraded secondary schools, the private sector institutions in both Japan and the Philippines accommodated most of the post-1945

Figure 5.4

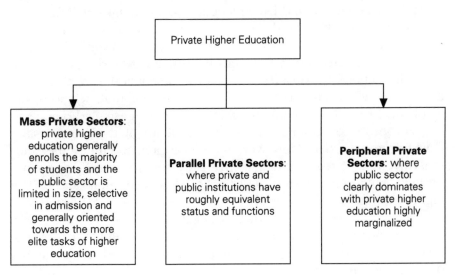

growth. Today, upon the heels of increasing Government regulation and, in Japan, of direct State support, efforts are underway to control private sector growth and development. These mass private systems have paid a price for their popularity. The initial diversity of institutional type and mission which characterized their formative years seems to have succumbed to the force of Government regulation and the lure of academic culture and prestige. Founding principles have been weakened or lost, and the multi-faculty, comprehensive university with all of its strengths and limitations is not the emulated model.

Mass sectors of private higher education also exist in such countries as Brazil, and Colombia where they respectively educate 63 and 59 per cent of all students enrolled in higher education. As in Asia, the private sector of higher education in these two Latin American countries functions in an environment where the public sector is limited in size, selective in admission and generally perceived to provide an education generally superior to that found in the private colleges and universities. Private higher education has also mushroomed in countries such as Korea, Argentina and Peru. In Korea and Argentina the private sector enrols approximately 77 and 91 per cent of the students respectively while in Peru private institutions now account for thirty of that nation's fifty universities (Utley, 1992).

Parallel private and public sectors in countries such as Belgium and the Netherlands represent a contrast to the elite public and populist private sectors of Japan, the Philippines, Colombia and Brazil. Historically drawing their sustenance from politically significant cultural groupings — such as the French and Dutch language communities of Belgium or the religious and ideological cleavages in the Netherlands — these institutions function in an environment where the letter and spirit of Government resources are deployed to ensure equality between private and public institutions. Universities, as we know, do not flourish with government funds alone and, as the strength of their cultural, religious and ideological roots has waxed and waned in an increasingly homogeneous European community, the founding values of these universities have become clouded. Moreover, in both Belgium and the Netherlands the Government regulation that invariably follows state support has further served to blur historical distinctions between public and private higher education. So powerful are the tendencies toward institutional homogeneity in the Netherlands and Belgium that observers are forced to ask if there is a true distinction between the public and private sectors; that is, do the private institutions enhance student choice and overall diversity in the system? In the Netherlands, where doctrinal differences between the Calvinists and Catholics have been supplanted by a broad sense of intellectual and religious tolerance, the answer appears to be no. In Belgium, where religious and language cleavages are much more evident, the situation suggests that private universities still reflect these separations and a distinct private sector therefore exists.

In Chile, with a private sector enroling about 37 per cent of all higher education students, a somewhat analogous situation of a parallel private sector exists. As Daniel Levey points out in his important book on private higher education in Latin America, *Higher Education and the State in Latin America: Private Challenges to Public Dominance* (1986), the homogeneity of Chile's private and public sectors of higher education have been forged from a base of public support for private universities. This similarity among Chile's private and public universities results from a gradual shift from full private financing to public subsidization. Because of this public support, Chile's private sector has come to resemble the public sectors of other Latin American countries. But what is particularly important with respect to Chile is Levy's conclusion that substantial equality exists in both prestige and quality between the private and public sectors. Chile has apparently achieved greater system-wide parity than has any other major Latin American nation with dual sectors; a parity that appears to approach what one would find in Belgium or the Netherlands. Even Chile's neighbour, Argentina, with considerable historical inclination to utilize centralized authority to guarantee institutional parity, has developed many clearly superior and inferior public universities. But in Chile, researchers such as Levy have generally concluded, even when allowing for great differences in institutional size, all eight universities enjoy considerable prestige. Moreover, the distinctions in quality that have emerged most prominently within Chile's eight universities are across the fields of study and disciplines rather than across institutions.

Examples of private higher education at the periphery are evident in countries such as France, Sweden, Canada and the United Kingdom — where dominant public systems have virtual monopolistic control over higher education. The scope of private higher education in these countries is largely determined by the extent to which the public sector is unable or unwilling to meet special demands. In France the thrust of private higher education is clearly centred on the *grand ecoles*, the specialized schools offering advanced professional training in such areas as engineering and business. In Sweden the prestigious state-supported but not state controlled Stockholm School of Economics is the lone remnant of a small but one-time flourishing private sector.

In Canada, Michael Skolnik, a Professor with the Higher Education Group at the Ontario Institute for Studies in Education, suggests that a few cracks are beginning to appear in traditional Canadian disposition to view higher education as a public monopoly. Canada, like many other countries, is quite supportive of private elementary and secondary education while taking a much more strident position when it comes to private higher education (Skolnik, 1987). In the United Kingdom, the University of Buckingham (founded in 1976) represents Britain's only private university. It must be pointed out, however, that the United Kingdom's more than forty-five ('traditional') universities formerly constituting the 'autonomous sector' under the old binary system, share many of the characteristics of the public and private universities of Belgium and the Netherlands just described.

Despite varying national conditions the private sectors of Sweden, France and the United Kingdom share common concerns — such as the inability of an academically competitive institution to support itself on tuition. Whether the support ultimately comes in the form of Government subsidies as in Sweden, or from the Roman Catholic Church as it does for several institutions in France, or from benefactors as in the United Kingdom, it is clear that private universities need substantial external support. Moreover, the peripheral private sector cannot seek to compete directly with the dominant public sector but must secure niches where it can reign substantially unchallenged. In France, for instance, the private sector serves over 32,000 students in universities while approximately 87 per cent of all business and 23 per cent of all engineering instruction takes place in the private *grand ecoles.*

In Mexico, where private higher education accounts for only about 15 per cent of the instruction, private institutions have carved out important niches in fields such as business, management and communications. More important, however, is the fact that graduates of Mexico's private universities usually get better jobs than their public counterparts — partly because they are better connected and partly because they are more highly educated. Nevertheless, the view is widespread that Mexico's private sector upholds, on balance, a higher quality than the public sector (Levy, 1986, pp. 114–70).

While these categories of mass, parallel and peripheral higher education seem to make sense when looking at higher education in a number of European, Asian and Latin American nations, they tend to break down in the United States — where the world's largest private sector enrols about three million students but less than 22 per cent of the nation's college and university students. Obviously a system of this size is not easily categorized. Collectively, American private higher education shares characteristics of the mass, parallel and peripheral sectors. However, unlike most of their overseas counterparts, America's private colleges and universities cannot simply be divided into those institutions providing more or different higher education. Benefitting from substantial, non-tuition external support, a small number of American private institutions seek to provide a better education than that found in the public sector.

It is not easy to examine private higher education from a cross-cultural perspective, and efforts in this area ought to take into account three basic factors identified by Clark, Geiger, Levy, Skolnik and others. First, the national environment: the political culture and values, the degree of national commitment or belief in the concept that market forces, competition and pluralism are fundamental tenets of educational policy must be considered. In addition, the role of and expectations surrounding higher education with respect to such the transmission of social, culural and economic values and their influence on the academic community's ethos must be part of any equation attempting to further our understanding of the role of private higher education. Second, the means by which private and public institutions divide the education turf. We must, for example, ask what types of institutions seek to increase access? What sector performs the elite functions? In what ways do the private and public sectors compete? In what ways do they complement each other? Finally, any cross-cultural examination must consider how higher education is actually conducted in each country. How have state action, administrative custom, national goals and financial resources placed their particular stamp on higher education?

The Arguments For and Against Private Higher Education

While the difficulty encountered in trying to characterize public and private higher education from a cross-cultural perspective is readily apparent, it is useful to examine some of the arguments for and against private sectors of higher education. When looking at these positions it is important to keep in mind that they are generally part of a much broader debate about the proper roles of the state and private organizations in a particular nation. That is, in the aggregate can (or do) private institutions provide elements essential to the character of a nation's makeup? In short, any discussion of privatization of higher education will most probably be part of a much broader national discussion regarding the advantages which private organizations provide for the attainment of state goals.[9]

The case for and against private and public sectors is effectively organized around four concepts and their attendant arguments are concisely and effectively outlined by Dan Levy: freedom; diversity; equity; and effectiveness.

Freedom, as Levy points out, has two major dimensions. One is institutional autonomy or freedom from unwarranted or excessive external control. The other is intellectual freedom, related to the latitude for constituents to express themselves without restraint from either outside or inside the institution. As Eric Ashby (1966) has pointed out, academic freedom is an absolute concept. It cannot vary with latitude, race, political sphere or national boundary (p. 321).[10] A nation without academic freedom cannot have free scholarship or superior universities. And today a nation lacking a strong and vibrant university system is at a certain worldwide economic disadvantage.

At one extreme, proponents of private higher education argue that freedom is afforded greater protection when the state is limited to areas unfeasible for private action. Private universities, less directly dependent upon public appropriations, provide an essential reserve protection at times when legislative or executive pressures on public institutions may become intolerable. Institutional autonomy and intellectual freedom are enhanced; and dangers of tyranny through monopolistic control or public politicization are minimized. This is not to suggest that private institutions are impervious to external pressures on orthodoxy — political or otherwise — but rather that private colleges and universities offer a certain degree of protection. While both public and private institutions have certain tendencies towards sycophancy, the patrons of these two types of institutions are often quite different. Opponents of private institutions are often less sanguine, arguing that such organizations are unduly tied to particular groups that demand their own form of orthodoxy. This implies that these groups broadly use power in ways that threaten both autonomy and intellectual freedom (this is an argument often used against church-related higher education in the United States — fundamental or mainstream). Still others assert that the state, recipient of public taxes and guardian of the national interest, has the major responsibility for providing the best service to its people and is therefore the logical, legitimate and perhaps the sole custodian of higher education. With regard to *diversity*, Levy points out that proponents of privatization argue that private colleges and universities are more responsive to societal needs, bring to a nation vital elements of pluralism by offering more adaptability, free choice, innovation and are less constrained by remote governmental *apparatchiks* and their political and cultural orthodoxy. Moreover, diversity suggests the existence of a range of institutions different from one another in the way they are managed, their perceptions of priorities, and the services they provide. This diversity implies the existence of a market where people seeking services (an education) can shop around and choose the institution best suited for their needs. The result is a wider range of institutions than would be financed by government alone. This provides students and their families with greater choice, potential employers as donors, professors and administrators who can commit themselves and their energies to a college or university that most meets their needs and aspirations. However, the educational market is not an entirely free one; as the costs of private services are likely to be higher than those provided by public institutions (Pifer, 1984, pp. 60–1). Nevertheless, at a minimum it is self-evident that dual sectors provide more choice and diversity than a single sector.

Public proponents, as Levy points out, offer the retort that private choice often alters public purpose, that policy choices need to be reached popularly, democratically, by consensus, or by the political powers or party leading the country. For those individuals, higher education is too important a national, social and economic priority to be left in the hands of private individuals and must be responsible and accountable as defined in the particular political arena of each State.[11]

Equity

Advocates of privatization often praise private universities for reducing excessive State subsidies based upon forced taxation of all citizens for a higher education which is only available to some. Beneficiaries of higher education argue that these adherents of privatization should pay their own way whenever feasible. If, for example, university attendance results in a higher lifetime income for an individual, why shouldn't that person pay a significant cost of his/her education? Why should an individual who does not attend a university — thus forsaking the economic benefits — be taxed to support the person who is gaining financial advantage by enroling? Less like minded individuals retort by pointing out that only the state can provide low cost and equal opportunity, thereby promoting equitable social and economic opportunity and progressive societal change. These same critics contend that private institutions are generally more accessible only to those with substantial economic resources, or who enjoy other special (social, political or religious) advantages. Thus it is argued that the existence of private higher education tends to create social, political or economic isolation — thereby perpetuating class distinctions.

Effectiveness

For academics and those directly concerned with the role of universities in a nation's economic and technological development, the most important aspect of the privatization debate often rests with effectiveness. Effectiveness relates to the economist's definition of efficiency — achieving maximum output from minimum input. Effectiveness also relates to a usage common in the literature on organization development — the ability of an organization to decide on realistic objectives, devise innovative strategies and define long-term goals to which constituents can commit themselves. There is, of course, no guarantee that private activity is actually in the public interest. The freedom of private institutions to choose their own goals can lead to redundant or wasteful disbursement. In short, effectiveness is directly related to the success of any university in achieving its particular goals.

Foremost among higher education's goals is academic quality; yet effectiveness also rests in the fulfilment of scientific, political, social, employment, economic, technological or other goals. As Levy suggests, private higher education partisans argue that autonomy, choice, diversity, pluralism, innovation, responsiveness, the ability to attract donors, student success, coupled with the benefits of competition (including competition between public and private universities) minimizes the prospect of academic stagnation and fosters educational effectiveness. Excellence, according to proponents of privatization, is best achieved through pluralism and market mechanisms which stimulate human activity and commitment, rather than through state mandates.

Less sanguine opponents respond that too much private activity in higher education leads to divisiveness and a sidestepping of the legitimate state role in seeing that higher education furthers national, social and economic goals. This control leads to a lack of coordination which ultimately dissipates human and economic capital. A related argument is that, while a diverse private higher education sector may have been appropriate for the relatively primitive and insular economies of states in the early nineteenth and twentieth centuries, the problems facing the interdependent and internationally competitive nations of the twenty-first century require greater centralization of resources and more unity to achieve productive and nationally integrating results. As Levy muses, opponents to the privatization of higher education believe building strong systems of higher education, like building strong nations, requires strong centralized state controls.

The emergence of private higher education also carries with it questions of quality assurance. How will institutional quality be monitored? What is the role of the state in quality assurance? Will voluntary institutional accreditation provide adequate quality assurance? Are the traditional processes for ensuring educational quality adequate? What types of new paradigms need to be considered? Questions such as these are difficult enough to address under any circumstances but with the exponential expansion of private higher education in parts of Asia and South America as well as its more modest growth in Eastern Europe they take on added importance. Research on quality assurance processes and its relationship to the expansion of private higher education internationally needs considerable attention.

Conclusion

The international debate regarding public and private higher education is both intellectually vibrant and relevant. Some nations debate the fundamental point of whether or not to allow private sectors of higher education, other nations consider the matter in terms of degree (the portion of higher education that should be privatized). A few nations sit on the sideline. Nations that regard private higher education as impossibly alien to their tradition or political system might be interested in knowing that privatization was widely regarded in the same way by such countries as Poland, Argentina and Nigeria. For nations such as Russia, Ukraine and China, beginning to experiment with efforts to interject aspects of privatization into their basic economies, one may wish to consider the extent to which this concept will ultimately carry over into higher education. Any extensive expansion of private higher education in those countries may seem highly unlikely but in a global economy where the quality, adaptability and effectiveness of higher education has a direct link to a nation's position in an increasingly technological and interdependent world stranger things can happen.

The appropriate questions regarding private higher education internationally may not be 'Will the need for a nation to infuse new life and vigour into its higher education system cause educational leaders to experiment with privatization?' but rather 'Can such countries, trying to recover from the constrictions of highly centralized planning and control, afford not to have a vibrant private sector of higher education?' and 'How will quality be assured?'. Not easy to answer, these questions represent the types of issues being raised as the privatization of higher education takes on increasing importance.

Notes

1 Lacking leading private research universities along the lines of Stanford, Chicago, Harvard and Princeton, the Japanese private sector remains totally overshadowed by such national universities as Tokyo and Kyoto. For some basic contrasts American and other systems of higher education see Bok (1986).
2 The Chronicle of Higher Education Almanac, 25 August 1993.
3 Cardozier (1987). The US Department of Education projects little fluctuation in the percentage of students enrolled in private higher education over the next ten years.
4 Clark raises these questions in the foreword to Geiger (1986), pp. xi–xiv.
5 In 1992 the Kirov Institute enrolled more than 6000 students, 3500 of whom attended on a full-time basis and they had a faculty and professional research staff of 550. About 70 per cent of its operating budget comes from the State and despite the hyper inflation gripping Russia the Institute's appropriation from the Government has increased only about 3 per cent a year over the past two years. There is considerable feeling among the faculty and administration of the Institute that privatization is necessary for their basic survival. Source: Interviews and discussions with faculty and administration at Kirov Institute, April 1992.
6 Interviews with staff of these academies, April 1992.
7 For a report on discussion regarding private higher education at a 1992 meeting of the International Association of Universities see Utley (1992).
8 In 1991/92 seven of the twenty top fund-raisers in US higher education were public universities: University of Wisconsin at Madison, University of

Minnesota, Indiana University, University of California at Berkeley, University of Washington, University of Illinois and the University of California at Los Angeles. An eighth institution, Cornell, while private is also the public land-grant University of New York. Source: *Chronicle Almanac,* 30.

9   Pifer (1984), pp. 55–6. See also Levy (1986) and Geiger (1986). For a provocative look at how public and private higher education interplay and competition fosters excellence in both sectors see Hollinger (1989).

10   Also see Berdahl (1971).

11   The contribution private higher education makes to diversity is not overlooked by government. The Statewide Plan for Higher Education in New Jersey reflects values resident in many state master plans when it states: 'It is through the diversity of sponsorship, purposes, programs, environment and size that independent (private) institutions proved students with a variety of options essential to freedom of choice in higher education. The State should . . . maintain an evenhanded fiscal policy . . . to insure that independent institutions have a chance to compete'. (Boyer, 1987, p. 4).

References

ASHBY, E. (1966) *Universities, British, Indian, African,* Cambridge, MA, Harvard University Press.

BERDAHL, R.O. (1971) *Statewide Coordination of Higher Education,* Washington, DC, American Council on Education, pp. 3–17.

BOK, D. (1986) *Higher Learning,* Cambridge, MA, Harvard University Press.

BOYER, E. (1987) *Excellence for Service: A Report by the Commission on the Future of Independent Higher Education in New Jersey.*

CARDOZIER, V.R. (1987) *American Higher Education,* Brookfield, VT, Avebury Press.

GEIGER, R. (1986) *Private Sectors in Higher Education, Structures, Function and Change in Eight Countries,* Ann Arbor, MI, University of Michigan Press.

HOLLINGER, D.A. (1989) 'Academic Culture at Michigan 1938–1988: The apotheosis of pluralism', in *Rackham Reports,* Ann Arbor, MI, University of Michigan, pp. 58–101.

LEVY, D.C. (1986) *Higher Education and the State in Latin America: Private Challenges to Public Dominance,* Chicago, IL, University of Chicago Press.

PIFER, A. (1984) *Philanthropy in an Age of Transition,* New York, The Foundation Centre.

SKOLNIK, M.L. (1987) 'State control of degree granting: The establishment of a public monopoly in Canada', in WATSON, C. (Ed) *Governments and Higher Education — The Legitimacy of Intervention,* Toronto, OISE, pp. 56–83.

UTLEY, A. (1992) 'Private fears, public worries', *Times Higher Education Supplement,* 27 November.

6   The Management and Mismanagement of School Effectiveness

Lynn Davies

Introduction

> It is essential to the triumph of reform that it shall never succeed. (William Hazlitt)

The idea of school effectiveness and the associated research is increasingly popular. There is a regular international conference series devoted to it, and an international journal. While much of the history of what we might term the 'school effectiveness movement' has been based in USA, Europe and Australasia, findings and ideas from other parts of the world are also now coming to the fore, as evidenced in Levin and Lockheed's recent collection *Effective Schools in Developing Countries* (1993). As they point out, the appeal of effectiveness research is that it is simultaneously sophisticated (statistically) and common sense. The factors associated with 'good' schools are rarely surprising, but it appears useful to have our hunches confirmed systematically to add weight to policy and management reform.

The major problem that has been acknowledged throughout the effectiveness research is that recognizing an effective school is not the same as creating one. Translating the lists of factors into school improvement in another context appears fraught with barriers. This chapter argues, however, that the crucial reason for the failure in school improvement programmes is that the political analysis has been ignored in favour of technical, material and organizational psychology questions. The very focus on 'variables in achievement' has been an insular and self-defeating process. School effectiveness research shoots itself in the foot every time it fails to analyze the function of schooling in what Fuller (1991) would term a 'fragile state'.

Let us take a mythical example. What would happen if *all* schools in a society became effective according to conventional definitions? Effectiveness is traditionally established by comparing schools on their examination successes in 'core' subjects such as mathematics, science and language. Effective schools are found to be those which have high expectations of *all* their students, and think that every child has potential to achieve. Supposing a society genuinely determined to spread the sucesses of its demonstrably good schools to all educational establishments, and put in enough materials, infrastructure, training and motivational incentives for teachers to raise significantly the formal achievement rates of students. More and more children would pass examinations. More and more children and parents would have high expectations of their futures. Demand for the next level of education would increase dramatically. Demand for jobs associated with high achievement at school and beyond would increase similarly. (This is a recognizable scenario in countries suffering from qualification inflation such as India.) *Really* improving school effectiveness in terms of full academic achievement for all would lead swiftly to a situation totally out of control, a sort of Jurassic Park where intelligent dinosaurs juggled for ascendancy in an environment completely unprepared for them. This chapter examines the management — and purposeful mismanagement — of 'effectiveness' at two levels, State and school, and goes on to propose alternative viable goals which are more honest reflections of political and school-level reality.

The Importance of School Ineffectiveness for the State

Much school improvement policy is founded on a myth. The myth is that everyone from the Government downwards would like school effectiveness, but that there are just too many material or attitudinal constraints on its implementation. In fact, governments do not want effective schools in the academic or even vocational sense. The last thing a fragile State wants is too many articulate, well-qualified students. England is a case in point. Every time the examination results show a rise in standards, powerful sectors within the Department for Education claim that standards of assessment must be falling and that more means worse. Universities simply raise the entrance requirements in over-subscribed areas. If graduates cannot get jobs, they are told it is because they have chosen the wrong subjects. Rarely is it acknowledged that our schools and teachers have become highly effective in educating children within the system that we have. The immediate response when the system appears too successful is to instigate immediate 'reforms', sidetracking schools and teachers onto other activities to diminish their efficiency. A recent desperate ploy has been to focus on league tables of truancy rates, so that instead of congratulating teachers on their successes within the National Curriculum, they can be blamed for juvenile crime and delinquency. Developing countries are often the focus for school improvement programmes because their systems appear very inefficient. Children do not all receive the education provided; there are high repetition and drop-out rates; there are high levels of teacher and student absenteeism; teaching materials are scarce and teachers untrained to use time positively. Yet taking the deeply cynical view, schooling in many developing countries is highly effective for what it is needed for. It provides avenues for the few to gain specialist knowledge while containing the mass in the myth of opportunity and promise. It is *essential* to have untrained teachers, inadequate buildings, a high emphasis on examinations but low examination pass rates, and a high attrition rate which appears random, or at least not the fault of Government, only of 'culture'. The presence of a few high achieving schools is indeed important, to indicate the possibility of success; but it is crucial not to have too many of these, otherwise the shaky pyramid of selection starts to bulge and crack. It would be the educational equivalent of the European beef mountain. A poor country needs academically effective schools like a hole in the head.

Such an analysis is of course not new, and goes back to educational reformers such as Carnoy and Illich in the 1970s. More recently, Fuller (1991) in his absorbing book *Growing Up Modern* convincingly demonstrates how the State wants to deepen the effects of mass socialization for its own legitimacy, but has a 'rocky romance' with the school, experiencing deep contradictions and conflicts in the attempt to impress a common moral order and work ethic. Yet this important macro-political analysis has rarely been acknowledged to the micro-level investigations of school effects. I argue that it is only if we fully take on board the duality of mass schooling and non-mass achievement as essential to the perpetuation of inequality and political power, that we can understand the so-called 'failure' of some school improvement programmes.

Levin and Lockheed (1993) do have as the fourth of their 'necessary inputs' to effectiveness 'the will to act', including political will:

> This type of leadership and mass mobilization may require nothing short of a mass social movement with charismatic leadership to overcome the inertia of the education system and traditional practices. (p. 14)

However, I argue that the problem is more than inertia; it is the vested interest in maintaining ineffectiveness and avoiding improvement. As Bennett (1993) comments with regard to Thailand:

'Because one of the stated functions of the school is to promote national unity, any departure from the National Curriculum tends to be highly suspect. Moreover, one of the unstated functions of the school is to maintain the existing socioeconomic order. Consequently, attempts of teachers to be involved with their students in larger local issues can lead to serious consequences. I have known several teachers in Thailand who have been driven out of the profession, or even killed, for such political activity. Thus, it is necessary to tackle the system as a whole rather than trying to take on the problems of individual schools . . . (p. 44)

If we are to provide effective schooling for poor and disadvantaged children, we must first show how this advances the political interests of those with power, or at the very least, how it benefits at least one powerful group. (p. 51)

Bennett shows how some threat is needed to achieve any real political change or change in the middle classes reaping the greatest benefit from schooling: in Thailand it was communist insurgency, in Nepal it was the continued public failure of previous projects, in Ghana it was the Government's need to show it was truly concerned with improving the life of the rural masses. Even there, one wonders how far innovation will be sustained when the political threat disappears.

It is time to recognize the ironies involved. Governments by and large love conventional effectiveness research — except for the international comparative studies showing differences between countries on, say, maths achievement. There was a time in the 1970s when effectiveness research was seen as highly suspicious by local authorities in UK, because it could show differences between schools within one authority and with very similar intakes; the preference for local authorities was to support traditional sociological research which demonstrated the importance of the family in determining educational achievement. However, national governments welcome the idea that similarly funded schools with similar 'intakes' can produce markedly different results. The focus on school 'climate' and 'whole school development' draws attention away from the effects of levels of poverty in the surrounding community or of the State funding of the school itself. If one school can be effective with limited resources, why not all? Hence teachers and headteachers can be fingered for the poor attainment of their pupils, and hereafter anything from unemployment to single parenthood.

This is not to say that there *are* no differences between schools in their management, organization, climate, nor that we should not try to research these and make schools nicer and more productive places for staff and students. My argument is with the larger-scale comparative studies which use multivariate types of analysis to produce statistical rankings of schools on a measure such as examination achievement. As soon as a league table is produced, there has to be someone at the bottom — even if that 'bottom' is created artificially by the research itself. What happens in reality is the same as with reading ages, or intelligence quotients: while they begin with being simple descriptions of the range of possibility, they take on a normative stance, so that 'below average' is seen as problematic rather than a function of the fact that on any measurement of a range, just below half the population has, by definition, to be 'below average'.

What occurs is a competition about competition — a double whammy. School success is rationed, so that not all pupils, by definition, can pass a selective examination, or even a supposedly criterion-referenced one such as 'A' level. Parents draw up all sorts of unofficial league tables for which primary schools manage to get children through a selective secondary entrance examination; yet of course if one school get more, another schools must get less. This zero-sum phenomenon is frequently misinterpreted in league table type research. In a ten-person race with only three medals, someone has to come tenth; making one runner more effective has to be at the expense of other runners. There is no way all can win — even if they are all faster than last year.

The same mythology is propounded by governments about what parents want. John Dewey's pronouncement 'what every good parent wants for his child, that should the community want for all its children' is based on a fundamental flaw. What parents want for their children in a competitive system is individual success. But individual rationality does not translate into collective rationality. While vocational education may be the most collectively rational for a society, it is not what parents want. Effective schooling research plays into the hands of this individual competitiveness, colluded with by governments concerned with their survival and popularity.

Thus while the philosophy of effective schooling research is seductively simple — identify a good school and spread the word — the whole charade is doomed to failure because of the inescapable logic of competition. Not all schools can be good, can win medals. In competitive systems, backed up by league tables and parental support, good schools get better and poor schools get worse. That is what market-oriented governments want, of course, but it is not efficient — or even humane.

Individual Maximization Through Inefficiency

School ineffectiveness is important too at the micro-level. Like governments, it is not necessarily that teachers and heads would dearly love to be effective but are constrained by inadequate materials or weak leadership. In communities where teachers make an important second living from private tuition, it is beneficial for formal schooling — or even their own classroom teaching — to be ineffective, so that parents must buy costly private lessons. As Reilly (1987) pointed out with regard to public sector administrators, it is essential for them to retain an inefficient system of nepotism, procrastination, authoritarian decision-making and lack of audit procedures if they are to maintain their interests and obligations and to demonstrate publicly their power and status.

One of the more interesting related theoretical fields developed in Scheeren's book on *Effective Schooling* is therefore *public choice theory.* This economic theory of the political process sheds light on the workings of public sector bureaucracies — of which schools are classic examples. The inherent tendency of bureaucracies towards inefficiency is explained by the principle of 'methodological individualism' (Van Mierlo, 1984, p. 59) whereby individuals and sub-groups within larger organizations have their own preferences and goals which do not necessarily coincide with overall organizational aims. Bureaucrats *choose* whether to be efficient or inefficient; the selective behaviour is the outcome of a trading process conducted within the informal structure of organizations, with subordinates purposefully behaving counter-productively, for instance as a signal of discontent to their superiors.

Goal displacement then occurs when the means of the organization (higher budgets, more staff, more activities, more management) become ends in themselves.

> The strong emphasis on internal maintenance functions and administrative leadership, as opposed to entrepreneurship and instructional leadership, could be interpreted as an example of goal displacement. In most educational systems the incentives for 'running a smooth ship', perhaps as an instrumental goal in safeguarding student enrolment, are much more in evidence than rewards and 'punishments' with respect to pupils' educational achievement. (Scheerens, 1992, p. 17)

In schools, then, as Boyd and Crowson (1985) claim, 'The needs of teachers and principals for control over their jobs most often takes precedence over the needs of individual children and their families' (p. 322).

Public choice theory appears to fit well with a notion I have developed elsewhere of 'maximization' — that actors in educational institutions will always seek to maximize the benefits to themselves of opportunities and changes in the organizational context (Davies, 1993). They will seek rewards — whether recognition, professional pride, money, self-esteem — from any situation, not all of which will be consonant with the expressed goals of the organization. Unless innovators attempt to work out what rewards everyone will officially and unofficially extract from a change, and indeed whether suitable rewards are available to all participants, the project is likely to fail. From the smallest child to the oldest serving member of staff everyone is able to act constructively in their own interest.

In theory, effective schools programmes should be attractive to most participants; children gain by achieving more, teachers gain more professional pride and respect, managers see a purposeful institution which reflects well on the leadership. Public choice and maximization theories nonetheless provide understandings of the subversion of the programmes. What can occur is displacement of the end-goals of effectiveness. The very nature of comparative effectiveness research is to 'isolate' a number of factors or means which good schools use. While there may be a close-meshed description of a good school, acknowledging the unique cultural climate and personalities which have generated success, the ultimate aim in the exercise is The Summary List. Hence another school cannot recreate the unique climate, but it can pick off items on The List. The tendency, therefore, is to focus on the means and forget the essential constant query about how they are implicated in the ends *for the school.* 'Frequent evaluation' or 'collegiate decision-making' become ends in themselves, rather than something which might in certain circumstances enhance student learning.

The second problem is that while achievement of the ends (satisfied customers) may appear uncontroversial, participants will still need to maximize for themselves the proposed means towards those ends. 'Strong leadership' may mean weaker power for other members. 'Imaginative teaching' requires thought and effort, with the results not instantly apparent. An 'orderly atmosphere' has little appeal on its own for children seeking excitement and relief from boredom. The trade-offs, exchanges and bargains people seek in institutional change are not always predictable. The only predictability will be that there will be a number of different 'rationalities' afloat.

The Seductions of Effectiveness Research

Ironically, effectiveness research may provide all sorts of rationales to support people's private agendas. A particular issue is researchers' stance with regard to 'intake'. As Angus (1993) comments:

> Family background, social class, any notion of context, are typically regarded as 'noise' — as 'outside' background factors which must be controlled for and then stripped away so that the researcher can concentrate on the important domain of school factors.

Such effectiveness research dehumanizes pupils — and teachers — by reducing them to 'intake variables': there is a cultural deficit, a stereotypical approach which appears to sympathize with the underachieving school for the 'poor quality' of its intake. The possibility that the definitions of 'achievement' and 'good intake' are organized in the interests of the ruling class, or of males, or of ethnic majority groups, is ignored. As the Congress of Manes in Brazil admitted:

> Our public schools are geared toward an ideal child. One who does not need to struggle for survival; who is well fed; who speaks the school's language, who knows how to handle a pencil and is capable of interpreting symbols, and who is stimulated by parents through all sorts of means. As this is not the reality of the Brazilian families, the schools do not have the right to impose these criteria, which are valid for the middle class, upon its students' majority. Its task is to educate Brazilian children as they actually are . . . (quoted in Leonardo, 1993, p. 75)

The 'value-added' approach of some effectiveness research — measuring what schools are able to add to base-line intake attainments — is better than league tables of culturally selective examinations attainment at one particular moment; but the message is still that dross must be converted to gold, that education can 'compensate' for society. This is what Fuller refers to as 'deepening the faith'. Yet reducing ethnic, gender and class inequalities and cultures to 'intake variables' which a school should compensate for rather than acknowledge the richness of, serves to the end only to consolidate the idea of cultural deficit. The State can blame the schools; but schools and teachers can, if pushed, still convincingly blame 'the home'.

Alternatives in Research and Policy

Unless more time and resources are spent chasing the unattainable and flawed goal of academically effective schooling for all, 'regardless' of intake, alternatives need exploration. One is for governments to 'come clean'. They could admit that higher levels of education, jobs and opportunities are rationed, and that the education system is a lottery — or at best a meritocracy. In some ways Japan does this quite successfully: there is little match between the *content* of schooling and eventual higher education or jobs, and success is accepted as the paper qualification and prestige of school attended, not what is learned (Inuit, 1993). There is no pretence that schooling prepares for work (except in *orientation* to hard work, competition and loyalty to the organization), or that more effective schooling would prepare more effectively. In a completely different way, Tanzania also has a semi-honest policy. State secondary schooling is severely rationed, and the political function of incorporation into the socialist ideology is openly adhered to. The problem there lies with the ideology of self-reliance conflicting with teachers' traditional ways of identifying success, so that agricultural activities can be ritualized and marginalized instead of being a key indicator of the effective school or successful student (Lwehabura, 1993).

A second option is to devise new forms of effectiveness research and resultant policy which acknowledge the realities of schools and cultures in different economic contexts (see Harber, 1992). Effectiveness indicators for schools with different stated goals (as in Tanzania) or different survival needs (as in Papua New Guinea; Vulliamy, 1987) throw interesting light on the way 'achievement' is defined and mediated through school processes. While there will be common management strategies between developed and developing worlds, there are marked divergences and creative skills needed in the latter; there is recognition that teaching and management are primarily jobs, not vocations, and that teachers are not just 'resources' or 'factors' in effective schooling but people with survival needs in their own right.

A third departure is to completely redefine the 'ends' to which mass formal education is geared. Countries have struggled long with vocational education, only to come up against the inexorable second place in the competition with existing academic qualifications and indicators of success (Sultana, 1992). Radical alternatives which aim at political conscientization can hit barriers at all levels of the State bureaucracy. For governments, as we have said, current inefficient formal education has a lot going for it. However, maintaining political order through schooling is still very expensive. More expenditure on education only means sacrifices in other parts of the economy. But what would happen if we looked more closely at the relationship between education and these other areas?

In theory, one could conceive of an education policy which could save money rather than squander it. The major expenditure for many countries is, for example, defence and internal policing. Logically, some initial expenditure on peace education would reduce the need for arms and vast defence forces — admittedly only effective if this were done internationally. Secondly, the still rising levels of population in many parts of the world have meant economies at breaking point — and barely able to keep education at its present level, let alone improve. Thus population education and family planning would appear crucial to reducing demands on the system and the resulting political instability. Thirdly, with or without population limitation, health expenditure is a major drain. If schools were measured as effective on the degree to which they turned out peaceable citizens with a concern for responsible parenthood and knowledge of health and nutrition, then the long-term survival of a country would be better assured.

Those peaceable, responsible citizens would, of course, have to do something and make a living. All the vocational literature seems to suggest that with fast changing technologies and cultures, skills are best learned on the job and not in expensive vocational institutions. The outstanding successes in non-formal education have been in functional literacy, where there is a purpose (other than certificates). Literacy in the many countries 'where there is nothing to read and no reason to write' (Bennett, 1993) may soon be forgotten and is a questionable sole priority. Schools would therefore focus best on very basic levels of literacy and numeracy as afternoon activities once the major national survival needs of peace, population and health had been covered.

These are admittedly very long-term and controversial visions, with education towards them requiring a surrounding cultural shift. It is unlikely that temporary governments will risk overt policies to prioritize such goals in schools, even if they make economic sense in the long term. Nonetheless, it is clear that unless new definitions of effectiveness are drawn up which are honestly attainable and economically sensible, the projects will come and go without any noticeable impact on a country's development.

An Existing Synthesis

There appear from all the above discussion three pre-conditions for a viable and honest effectiveness programme.

(i)   the desired 'outputs' cannot be success in competitive exam-
       inations;
(ii)   the material inputs and the learning outputs cannot be threaten-
       ing to fragile governments, and must be popular with parents;
(iii) the scheme must maximize the 'rewards' of teachers and
       headteachers.

There are few models available which fulfil all three of these criteria. One hopeful example is the New School programme for rural primary edu-cation in Colombia, presented at the World Conference 'Education for All' and described by Colbert, Chiappe and Arboleda (1993). This departs radically from conventional notions of age-grading, regular or routine timetabling and teacher transmission models. It uses self-instructional materials to be used individually and in study groups; the interesting angle is that teachers also are trained by the same independent, active learning means. There is a flexible promotion system to allow students to advance to another level at their own pace, or to leave school tempor-arily to help in agricultural activities. Parents and community members are mobilized for involvement; children are encouraged to apply what they learn in the community, participating in health, sanitation and nutrition activities. Significantly for management purposes, educational administration is focused on 'orienting rather than controlling', with administrative 'agents' required to integrate pedagogical practices with their administration.

That the scheme is truly radical is revealed in the tenor and choices within the evaluations.

> . . . the level of creativity among students of New Schools where
> a teacher is responsible for several grade levels does not differ
> significantly from rural schools where there is a teacher as-
> signed to each grade . . . children in the New School programme
> were found to have a much higher level of self-esteem . . . the
> fact that the self-esteem of girls equalled that of boys is particu-
> larly important; more participatory classrooms appear to help
> girls' self-esteem . . . in tests of socio-civic behaviour, self es-
> teem, and selected subjects (mathematics, Spanish), New School
> children scored considerably higher than those in traditional
> rural schools (Colbert *et al*, pp. 63 and 64)

It is indicative that subject competence appears last on the list, with cre-ativity and self-esteem featuring strongly beforehand. In terms of edu-cation for development in the present fast-changing world, autonomous and confident citizens will be far more 'effective' in their future contribution than will high-achieving curriculum role learners.

The project is interesting for our purposes also in the discussion of what happens in mass expansion. As argued earlier, it is relatively easy and non-threatening to have a scattered number of effective schools. Hence the success of small projects, experimental institutions and schools relying on a particular inspired head to turn them round. Expanding the New School project to 27,000 rural schools inevitably meant losses of consultation and a reduction in effectiveness and efficiency, with difficulties in timing the various training and materials elements to coincide. However, moves towards decentralization will help restore the quality approach, and there is a climate in which errors are admitted and even the third stage of going nationwide is recognizable as '*learning* to expand' (Korten, 1980, my emphasis) — that is, a tentative and self-correcting process rather than a technical procedural expansion.

The Management of Productivity

The Colombian example underlines what is the key to any discussion of school effectiveness: what constitutes 'achievement' and hence its assessment. I would like to contrast the 'conventional' measures of productivity and their management with those implied by schooling which would genuinely be effective for as many as possible. Scheerens (1992), for example, talks of the 'achievement-oriented school' which wants the highest possible teaching results. This sounds generalizable to any type of national or local goal, until one looks at the school policies he outlines:

> recording annual 'attainment' figures in terms of percentages admitted to various types of follow-up education, average test and examination results, data on drop-outs . . . employing achievement pressure as a criterion when recruiting new teaching staff . . . (p. 87)

> making more use of standardized school progress tests within the framework of whole school evaluation . . . (p. 90)

As argued in section 2 of this chapter, such emphasis on increasing the achievement of one school can, in a selective, competitive and pyramidal education system, only be bought at the expense of another school. The clear focus on 'strong leadership' that emerges from these criteria is always leadership *within* the school, rarely the community or regional leadership which can coordinate efforts rather than make schools compete against each other in inevitably biased races. 'Drop-outs' are black marks in the school profile rather than children with the sense to realize the dice are loaded against them, or who, as in the Colombian example, are temporarily or permanently engaging in productive activities within the community. 'Standardized' testing rarely means genuinely criterion-referenced and diagnostic skill-based evaluation, but a way of measuring children against some 'norm' by which by definition half are below average and inevitably deliberately or unconsciously stigmatized.

It is time school effectiveness literature moved away from the focus on strong leadership. As I have argued elsewhere (Davies and Gunawardena, 1992), this often has all sorts of masculinist connotations in its extraction of 'traits' associated with strength and the use of power — in spite of noises made about collegiate relationships and loose coupling. Yet the gendered notions of leadership are but part of a wider ideology which has accepted for far too long that education is like sport, and shares the same combative values. Teams can be built, but only to defeat other teams. The key to football success is always the team manager or the coach, distanced from the players in the way that conventional strong heads are those with the vision that separates them from their workaday staff or students. Even Scheerens admits that 'internally, educational leadership implies a certain depreciation in the professional autonomy of teachers' (p. 89). Leonardo (1993) in her fascinating comparison of a democratic and a conventional school in Brazil, found the Principal of the conventional school having exclusive decision-making powers; teachers were isolated and applied different literacy methods, getting together only to devise the final exams. In contrast, the democratic school was part of a state project of the Democratic Labour Party which created Integrated Centres of Public Education with distinct philosophies about integrated curricula, literacy methods and a critical approach to pedagogy and knowledge. There is no mention of 'leadership' in the latter account; presumably because all staff knew and understood the philosophy. 'Although staff meetings were usually headed by the Principal, Vice-principal, or a Coordinator, all proposals and problems were discussed and strategies adopted by a vote of the teachers' (Leonardo, 1993, p. 80).

Conventional school effectiveness management models, where effectiveness is defined as success in competitive achievement have lists of internal management factors which promote this. There is nothing wrong with many of the ideas, because of course enabling people to work at anything — whether group sewing circles or producing baked beans — requires the same sensitivity to their need for rewards, recognition or consultation. The list will include delegation, collegiate relationships, staff development, incentives, clear discipline policies and so on; but the essence of this management is still, as in sport, a *training* model. Schools are for training children to achieve; staff are trained to train them. Everyone may be institutionally happy and productive; but at the national level only some teams can win.

In contrast, effective schools which *in combination and co-operation* help the economy — rather than just support brittle governments and class elites — would have a management model which went beyond training, which was truly *educational* management. (There are often debates as to whether there is any real difference between education and training; the clear example I always give is to raise a question: 'You wouldn't mind your child having sex *education*; but . . .')

The goals of such education — what I shall call 'authentic-effective' — are four-fold: skills, empowerment, self-esteem and social responsibility. The move away from testing does not mean there should not be evaluation of school success. Skills are measured by amount of progress of various groups through criterion-referenced, graded assessments, not by competitive exams or age-standardized tests. Empowerment can be measured by the extent and way in which pupils and staff are able to participate in school and community decision-making together with the know-how to engage in autonomous study and to help others to study. Self-esteem is assessed in qualitative ways such as group discussion, as well as quantitative attitude scales. Social responsibility can be measured at school level by actual behaviour and behavioural incidents as well as by attitude questionnaires. National evaluations would include long-term tracer studies of future occupational productivity and family health as well as evaluations of participation in the sociopolitical infrastructure and behaviour with regard to social cohesion and population growth.

There is by definition no one management model which is linked to these goals; one can merely outline likelihoods, based on studies of non-conventionally 'effective' schools.

(i) To achieve empowerment and self-esteem, management is likely to be non-hierarchical and non-competitive. Teachers do not compete against each other for promotion, but gain rewards through recognition of their efforts with students on the four areas above. While there will be designated managers, these are coordinators, not leaders; decision-making and programme design will be in the hands of teachers.

(ii) Equity is not disguised as 'opportunity' but operationalized as efforts towards social justice. Schools do not bemoan their 'poor intake' as if this were a misfortune, but accept a range of cultural and learning backgrounds as normal. Monitoring is done to check the progress of groups such as females or ethnic minorities, not to rank individuals.

(iii) Organization is likely to be flexible. Students may come in and out of the programme, and timetabling and grading is for the benefit of pupils, not some internal notion of standardization, organizational efficiency and cost-effectiveness. Teachers, too, agree flexibility to suit their own professional and family needs. This is an honest and systematized flexibility, not a forced one where the school attempts a rigid routine timetable which then has to stigmatize students as drop-outs or truants and staff as absentees.

(iv) The organizational structure will match the desired political orientation which is to be one outcome of effective schooling. If this is some form of democracy, the school will have a democratic structure, with elements such as a School Council, rotational and elected positions for staff and students, different fora for participants to practice their articulation of views, the encouragement of debate and critical questioning of the school as well as of the national system.

(v) Teacher training and management training follow the same pedagogical principles as will need to be followed in the school: autonomous study, criterion-referenced assessment, participation in the decision-making of the institution, cooperation learning, and equitable treatment as adult co-learners.

There *are* examples of such authentic-effective schools and management strategies in various parts of the world. When they are individual ones, such as in the UK, they have to fight against the weight of Government policy and conventional acceptance of competition. When they have backing from the State — as in Brazil, Colombia, Denmark and more recently Portugal — their success and recognition is of course likely to be higher. The lessons that are learned from the management of state-backed effectiveness programmes is that while they will create change more realistically and quickly than localized initiatives, they must follow the same management principles as the system and outcomes they are trying to create: empowerment of participants in all stages of the change process; viewing change as a process of learning at all levels, not implementation strategy from expert to amateur;

consultation and openness about error and ignorance. Tanzania had well-known problems with its self-reliance strategies because of the mismatch between the vision and the way it was implemented: because of the transmission model of innovation, that is, the lack of consultation and participation, teachers never became self-reliant in self-reliance.

The management of school effectiveness can in the end only work through a nationally holistic and internally consistent approach, if it is not to be pseudo-effectiveness or pocket-effectiveness. Otherwise it is like pretending to have comprehensive schools when there are still grammar schools in the locality. As David Coleman, the sports commentator, enthused '. . . as they come through absolutely together, with Wells in first place . . .'

References

ANGUS, L. (1993) 'The sociology of school effectiveness', *British Journal of Sociology of Education*, 14, 3.

BENNETT, N. (1993) 'How can schooling help improve the lives of the poorest?', in LEVIN, H. and LOCKHEED, M. (Eds) *Effective Schools in Developing Countries*, London, Falmer Press.

BOYD, W. and CROWSON, R. (1985) 'The changing conception and practice of public school administration', in *Review of Research in Education*, 9, pp. 311–73.

COLBERT, V., CHIAPPE, C. and ARBOLEDA, C. (1993) 'The new school program; More and better education for children in rural areas in Colombia', in LEVIN H. and LOCKHEED, M. (Eds) *Effective Schools in Developing Countries*, London, Falmer Press.

DAVIES, L. (1993) *New Developments in Educational Management*, Paris, IIEP.

DAVIES, L. and GUNAWARDENA, C. (1992) *Women and Men in Educational Management: An International Inquiry*, Paris, IIEP.

FULLER, B. (1991) *Growing Up Modern: The Western State Builds Third World Schools*, New York, Routledge.

HARBER, C. (1992) 'Effective and ineffective schools: An international perspective on the role of research', *Educational Management and Administration*, 20, 3, pp. 161–9.

INUIT, A. (1993) 'The competitive structure of school and the labour market: Japan and Britain', *British Journal of Sociology of Education*, 14, 3.

KORTEN, D. (1980) 'Community organization and rural development: A learning process approach', *Public Administration Review*, 40, 5, pp. 480–511.

LEONARDO, A. (1993) 'CIEP: A democratic school model for educating disadvantaged children in Brazil', in LEVIN, H. and LOCKHEED, M. (Eds) *Effective Schools in Developing Countries*, London, Falmer Press.

LEVIN, H. and LOCKHEED, M. (Eds) (1993) *Effective Schools in Developing Countries*, London, Falmer Press.

LWEHABURA, J. (1993) '*School effectiveness and self-reliance in Tanzania*', unpublished PhD thesis, University of Birmingham.

MIERLO, J. VAN (1984) 'The economic theory of the political process and representative democracy', in *Maandscrift Economie*, 48, pp. 255–85.

REILLY, W. (1987) 'Management and training for development: The Hombe thesis', in *Public Administration and Development*, 7, pp. 25–42.

SCHEERENS, J. (1992) *Effective Schooling: Research, Theory and Practice*, London, Cassell.

SULTANA, R. (1992) *Education and National Development: Historical and Critical Perspectives on Vocational Schooling in Malta*, Malta, Mireva.

VULLIAMY, G. (1987) 'School effectiveness research in Papua New Guinea', in *Comparative Education*, 23, 2 pp. 209–23.

7   Failed Matrimony: Educational Projects and Their Host Institutions

Fiona Leach

The message about development assistance coming out of the major agencies has changed considerably over the past decade, not least in the education sector. Central to their current message is a shift from talk of the project as a major focus of the development initiative (with discussion revolving around ways of improving its success rate and impact) to talk of broader sectoral support and in particular support for locally-generated policy reform and local capacity-building. Some of the fashionable buzz words in the corridors of donor power these days are 'capacity-building', 'local ownership', 'sustainable growth' and 'policy analysis'. Where a sector-wide capacity-building approach has been in evidence for some time now in aid to rural development, it is relatively new to educational aid, where the free-standing project has been the dominant vehicle of assistance for the past twenty-five years. As it is, the debate over issues relating exclusively to the project process in education have now been put on the back burner. The talk is all of broad support to the whole education sector or to sub-sectors such as basic education, non-formal education or higher education. While no one is suggesting that the project should be killed off (it remains far too convenient a form of aid disbursement to donors), it is currently seen as having had a rather disappointing record, except where it has been supported by system-wide reform.

The project first became popular with donors in the 1960s because it was seen as an attractive alternative to programme aid, which was the earliest form of post-colonial development assistance. Programme aid suffered from a lack of accountability and high levels of 'wastage'. In contrast the project was a visible and well-defined entity, particularly suited to infrastructural support, for example, the construction of phys-ical facilities like hospitals, science laboratories and college buildings, and the purchase of equipment (thus incidentally boosting the donor countries' exports). Progress could be supervised and recorded by ex-patriate personnel who were directly responsible to the donor. In the case of bilateral aid, the potential high profile of the project appealed to politicians who needed to provide convincing evidence to their tax-paying voters back home that aid money was well spent. And above all, the project had (or was supposed to have) clearly specified finite objectives which allowed donors to see some clear outcomes while only making short term commitments to individual governments. These were typically of three to five years in the first instance, with the possibility of further extensions. Project aid was seen as altogether more 'manageable' than programme aid.

Over the past few decades, the commitment to the project by donors has been considerable, with a major proportion of aid disbursement being in the form of projects or technical assistance (much of which is linked to projects). However, despite the heavy commitment, disillusionment with the project has built up during the 1980s to the point where its reputation must be considered seriously tarnished in all sectors. There is increasing awareness and concern that projects have failed to stimulate long-term sustainable development to the extent anticipated in the early optimistic years of post-war development assistance (Verspoor, 1993; King, 1992). While projects are not necessarily doomed to failure, in most cases there have been too few lasting successes for them to have had a serious impact on national systems and individual successes have all too often proved difficult to replicate on a wider scale. The record of failure is highest in the poorest countries towards which much of the development assistance has been directed, and where it is most needed. Most of these countries are in Sub-Saharan Africa. Failure has been in large part attributed to the constraints that political and economic circumstances impose on project performance, and to the limited absorptive capacity for aid in many of these countries.

As economic decline during the 1980s has eaten into government spending on public services in the poorest countries, it has become increasingly apparent that the project is an artificial creation, an oasis of plenty (designed, resourced and staffed by the donor) in a desert of deprivation (located in resource-starved ministries or other public institutions). Often the donor has seen fit to set up a project implementation unit to oversee the project process; hence the term 'enclave' project (King, 1992, among others). As local institutional capacity has declined, so has dependence on donors increased for personnel, equipment, supplies and funds to meet recurrent project costs. And with it has receded the possibility of long-term sustainability of project activities and their internalization and/or replication within the relevant sector. This applies not least to education projects, where there is the additional factor that project outcomes are particularly difficult to assess due to their complex and not easily quantifiable goals and the large numbers of people involved (officials, teachers, trainers, students etc). All of this has fuelled the argument for a return to programme aid, in the form of a broader sectoral support to education (Verspoor, 1993; Colclough and Lewin, 1993).

Current strategies for broad programmes of support to education (as to other sectors) still try to preserve the level of accountability and 'finiteness' that initially made the project so attractive. This is being done firstly by releasing funds in tranches conditional upon a satisfactory level of performance in each phase. Secondly, educational aid is being increasingly linked to policy reform in education (this might be, for example, a diversion of resources from higher to basic education, increased private financing of education, or a reduction in non-teaching staff). Thirdly, aid is being increasingly tied up with structural adjustment agreements on economic reforms (market liberalization, privatization, removal of subsidies etc), or with other forms of conditionality such as evidence of good governance, cuts in defence spending and an improved record on human rights.

Projects remain an important tool for aid disbursement, but they are now to come under the umbrella of the sectoral or sub-sectoral programme (and will, in theory at least, be financed strictly according to the objectives of that programme and less according to donor priorities or available expertise). In the (sub)sectoral programme, the emphasis now is on getting the policy 'right' and helping governments to reach this 'right' policy through their own analytical capacity, while at the same time taking more responsibility for development initiatives. This has profound implications for the project process which have not yet been fully explored, and which I touch on in this chapter.

King (1992) raises the issue in a recent paper by suggesting that these new perspectives on aid will require a dramatic shift of paradigm for the aid community, one that will prove to be as demanding for donors as it will be for recipients.[1] Indeed, the emphasis being placed on local capacity-building and local ownership of policies, programmes and projects will require a new approach to project activity at all stages — at the planning, design, implementation and evaluation stage — one which must involve local implementers or beneficiaries (who are not always the same) throughout, with a view to their taking control of the whole process as soon as possible. While governments may well learn to formulate their own 'sensible' policies for any one sector (with no doubt more than a little 'ventriloquization' from donors) and from these to determine their own priorities for external aid, they still have to implement the policies and the projects conceived within the new policy framework.

It is with this in mind that I propose in this chapter to look inwards on the project once again, unfashionable though this might be in the current donor climate. In particular I should like to examine in the sober light of day, away from the artificially bright offices where aid policy is made, the grim and often ignored reality of what goes on during project implementation, especially in the poorer countries of Africa where infrastructure and expertise are low but where aid activity is usually at its most intense. I shall then suggest that one important but largely ignored reason for the poor success rate of projects can be found in the nature of the project itself, which makes its developmental goals of capacity building and local ownership difficult to achieve (for these goals have always been there, but have often been sidetracked by the donors' 'quick fix' approach).

To look at the project in operation, I propose to adopt an analytical tool which appears to have been rarely used in the context of Third World development, namely the concept of the 'organizational culture' (one exception is Franks, 1989). This suggests that organizations belong to different cultures (not in any national or ethnic sense, although an extensive cross-national study by Hofstede (1980) indicated that different nationalities show preference for different organizational cultures), and as a result operate according to a different set of dynamics. They have different goals, different timescales and different types of power structure, roles and tasks. Their personnel have different expectations, preoccupations, personal agendas and work patterns. An analysis of the project, and the host institution into which it is usually introduced, shows that each belongs to a different organizational culture. My thesis here is that there is an inherent incompatibility between the two (the 'failed matrimony' of the title of this chapter), which originates in these organizational differences. Unfortunately, as my analysis will show, this incompatibility renders the project counter-developmental insofar as it decreases rather than increases capacity within the local institution. While on the one hand it may reach its stated short-term objectives, the internal dynamics of the project prevent it from meeting the longer-term development objective of local institutionalization and sustainability.

Almost all education projects are based in government institutions in the host country. This may be a Department in the Ministry of Education (for example, the planning section, the curriculum development centre or the adult education unit), or an educational institution (for example, a university faculty, a college of teacher education or a vocational training centre). A number of employees of the Ministry or other institutions, who will normally be civil servants, will be seconded to work on the project. In poorer countries of Africa and Asia they will usually work alongside one or more resident expatriates employed by the donor or executing agency on one or two-year contracts. In the more developed countries of Asia and North Africa, where more local expertise is available, resident expatriates may be less common, and instead the project agreement will allow for a series of short-term external consultants to visit the project to monitor progress or give professional advice and support. While some educational projects are concerned exclusively with infrastructure (constructing buildings or providing equipment) it is more usual for them to include an institution-building component. For this to be realized, and for the project to be viable in the long term, the counterparts who are assigned to work with the expatriates are required to learn from the latter and gradually take over their roles and responsibilities, to the point where they can run the project alone, and the activities and procedures initiated by the project become absorbed into the routine of the host institution.

One of the most interesting writers on 'organizational cultures', and one of the most influential in the literature on organization and management, is Charles Handy, whose book *Understanding Organisations* (first published in 1976) is a classic in its field. More recently he has applied his ideas on organization to the school (1986). Crucial to an analysis of the culture of an organization is a consideration of its informal as well as its formal structures and procedures, namely those that relate to interpersonal interactions, group dynamics, levels of motivation etc. The significance of informal structures and procedures in organizations has been well researched in Western management literature, for example as early as the 1920s in the famous American Hawthorne studies (Roethlisber and Dickson, 1939), but, strangely, little research of this nature has been undertaken in Third World institutions (some exceptions are Hyden, 1983; Moris, 1977; Heaver, 1982; Reilly, 1987, none of whom, however, is writing about educational institutions). Yet an analysis of informal structures is crucial in that it shows how individuals seek to realize their own personal ends within the workplace by means of informal agendas which often do not coincide with the official aims of the organization. This is particularly pertinent in the context of institution-based aid projects in developing countries.

Empirical support for the incompatibility between the project and the host institution is provided by a number of aid projects in Northern Sudan which I studied in depth between 1986 and 1989. Four of these projects were based in educational institutions, namely a training college for agricultural technicians, a postgraduate university institute, an English language institute and an English language support unit within a college of higher education. All the projects involved two or more expatriates, who were employed as project managers, consultants or heads of department, and who worked with a number of Sudanese occupying positions of Director or Assistant Director, Head of Department, lecturer or teacher in the host institution. Most of the Sudanese were assigned as counterparts to the expatriates.

Although Handy is writing essentially about Western industrialized settings, his work provides a useful starting point for a cross-cultural exploration. I intend to adopt some of his concepts and categories in the discussion that follows. I shall start with an analysis of the project and the host institution as 'organizational cultures' and then within this framework look at the different power sources, leadership styles, types of motivation and psychological contracts that prevail within the two kinds of organization, in order to highlight the inherent incompatibilities which undermine the capacity of the project to generate innovation and development in the host institution.

Organizational Cultures

Handy (1985) talks of organizations conforming to four basic 'cultures' or ideologies, each with its own structures, values, customs, traditions and unwritten rules. These are the power culture, the role culture, the task culture and the person culture. Within this model, the Sudanese educational institutions like most public institutions in developing countries resembled, in form if not in substance, role cultures. In other words, they were large bureaucratic pyramid-like organizations, with well-established rules and procedures, a rigid hierarchy, centralized decision-making and well defined roles for individual employees, who are not expected to perform over and above what are clearly laid down as their duties. In a role culture the organization is engaged primarily in systems maintenance, so that it is slow either to acknowledge the need for change or to carry out change even when this is perceived as necessary. Within the present context it is usually poor in resources, which also militates against change.

In many Third World institutions, the role culture has been fused with, and in some cases superseded by, a power culture. A power culture according to Handy is dominated by a central figure with great power and influence who personally chooses those who work around him/her. Lines of communication always lead to the centre and all the most important decisions are taken by the central figure. Companies set up by exceptionally motivated individuals with strong personalities, like Ford or Rockefeller in the USA, Beaverbrook, Rowland and Maxwell in the UK are, at least while their creators remain alive, power cultures. In the context of public institutions in developing countries, individuals in powerful positions maintain their control not by ensuring that rules and procedures are followed and by exercising judicious use of rewards and sanctions (as in role culture), but by political patronage, kinship allegiances and the trading of favours (Hyden, 1983). Anyone with experience of working within a large government institution in a developing country will recognize these characteristics.

Into this combined role and power culture (the host institution) is introduced a task culture (the project), which is of a fundamentally different nature. To Handy, the whole emphasis of the task culture is on getting the job done, and individuals work single-mindedly towards this end. The project is comparatively rich in resources, and its personnel (expatriates) are selected on their ability to perform quickly and competently as members of a tightly-knit team. The individual is considered more important than the role he/she is given, as roles may have to be adapted to fit new circumstances; the individual must be flexible if he/she is to achieve the pre-determined objectives within the specified time limit. Nothing is static or unchangeable. The task culture is essentially a short-term injection of resources designed to generate significant change in the system. Team members earn respect on the basis of performance rather than age or status, as is found in a role culture.

Expatriates have usually passed through a recruitment process designed to hand-pick candidates on the basis of knowledge, experience and ability to work in a task culture. On the other hand, their local counterparts have usually been coopted to work on the project not because they show any particular aptitude in a task culture but because they happen to be in relevant positions in the host institution, indeed they may be the only individuals available. Moreover, most if not all of their work experience will have been in a highly bureaucratic environment dominated by a combined role and power culture.

This brief description of Handy's categorization of organizational cultures serves to reveal a potential incompatibility between the host institution and the project in terms of momentum, aims, strategies and time scales. In addition, personnel will have different terms of reference and different priorities, which may be a source of conflict. Although seconded to the project, often with specific job descriptions, counterparts will probably still operate according to the terms of reference provided by their institution (and in some cases have to carry out their regular institutional duties as well as those demanded by the project). This means that their perception of what should be appropriate roles and workloads does not usually change. Moreover each side owes allegiance to a different employer, one to the host institution and the other to the donor. It is not surprising therefore that tensions occur on projects over expectations as to what each side should do.

While it is not unusual for different branches of an organization to subscribe to different cultures (for example, departments of planning, finance, training or research), it is important that they are integrated within a unified and coherent structure working towards broad common institutional goals. In the case of the project (a product of Western organizational thinking) and the host institution (subscribing to a different set of social and organizational norms), they are not integrated and are not working towards common goals. On the Sudanese projects, although the expatriate project manager shared a coordinating role with the local counterpart (usually the project co-manager), in practice the project and the host institution functioned as two separate entities, with the former controlled by the project manager, who only needed to liaise with his/her counterpart on issues which concerned local staff and host government procedures for which the latter was responsible. In addition, because they were preoccupied by the need to meet project targets on time and saw that their counterparts worked at a slower pace, the expatriates tended to assume responsibilities and duties which should have been shared with, and gradually passed on to, their counterparts. This applied to both specialist tasks (for example, curriculum development, manpower planning) and to general administration. Overall, it served to aggravate the project's isolation from its host organization and to reduce the interdependence of organizational structures and processes which was necessary for long-term project sustainability.

From the above discussion, we can see that there are already potential difficulties between the project and the host institution, stemming from their conflicting organizational cultures. These difficulties are multiplied once the project is placed in a bicultural setting, where it remains essentially a product of Western concepts and design but has to operate from a base inside a Third World institution which is faced with chronic problems of resourcing and infrastructure to a degree not usually experienced in the West, and which subscribes to a very different set of norms and values. In addition, there may well be further, culture-based, areas of incompatibility and conflict between the two groups working on the project (expatriates and nationals).

Power and Decision-making

The way that power is exercised and decisions made within the different organizational cultures also has important implications for the institution-building capacity of projects. Different organizational cultures make use of different types of power, or different combinations of power. Those that typically dominate in the role/power culture (host institution) and the task culture (project) indicate that, when combined, they are largely counterproductive for long-term development goals.

Handy (1985) identifies six power sources available in organizations. These are physical power, resource power, position power, expert power, personal power and as an important counterforce to these there is 'negative power', which is the (illegitimate) power to disrupt or delay. On a typical project, a number of power sources are available to the expatriates. They usually wield high expert power and considerable resource power (on behalf of the donor). In theory this resource and expert power is counterbalanced by local management's position power, based on its official status and its right to enforce rules and procedures. However, in practice, in much of Africa at least, this power is eroded because it is not backed by a willingness to enforce discipline and accountability, by consistent support from above or by adequate resource or expert power.

This erosion of resource and position power and the absence of high levels of expert power are compensated for by an arbitrary brand of personal power which stems from the power culture. This is less the power of a charismatic individual, as Handy sees it (although that may also be an ingredient), than the power which derives from patronage and political or kinship allegiance. Unfortunately such power does not usually work in the interest of official organizational goals.

At the same time, in many government institutions the general lack of recognizable managerial skills (with individuals promoted to management positions largely on seniority rather than on ability or experience), the high level of apathy which generally prevails, and the fact that many combine their Government posts with other occupations such as consultancy work, private teaching or business, means that it is unlikely that local management will make full use of even the limited position power it retains, unless core interests are at stake. Indeed this was the case on the projects studied, where the project manager was left with a potentially disproportionate share of managerial power on the project, which served to weaken what little management ability existed on the local side at the start of the project. And yet the development of local managerial capacity is a crucial ingredient of institution building and local ownership.

It can been seen therefore that the way that power is practised and decisions made on aid projects is potentially dysfunctional and counter-developmental. In particular, on the projects studied the expatriates' excessively strong operational power base and local management's indulgence in personal power to compensate for its weakened authority were sources of considerable friction between the two sides. In addition the spasmodic use of negative power as a blocking mechanism by nationals (for example, withholding information, using delaying tactics, misinformation and even sabotage), while being largely an expression of resentment at the excessive power wielded by the expatriates, was nevertheless a harmful force which served to reduce project effectiveness. The end result was that the expatriates exercised increasing control over the project process and local staff were marginalized and ignored. This is quite the opposite of what is intended on a development project.

Leadership

Because of the perceived lack of local managerial expertise, many expatriates are placed in leadership or managerial positions, even if officially they have only been appointed as advisers or consultants (Stutley, 1980). Much has been written about the nature of leadership in organizations. Some writers of what is called 'contingency theory' identify different leadership strategies or styles for different situations (or contingencies) (for example, Vroom and Yetton, 1973; Fiedler, 1967; Schein, 1980; Hersey and Blanchard, 1982). Handy (1985) talks about various leadership models but Hersey and Blanchard's situational leadership model is potentially the most useful for our current analysis. This proposes a continuum of styles ranging from an authoritarian/ bureaucratic style which is suitable for what they call 'low maturity' followers, i.e., those lacking in skills, motivation and confidence, through a more participative style to a hands-off delegating style suitable for 'high maturity' followers who are skilled, motivated and competent. In weak institutional environments, such as those that prevail in many developing countries, a strongly directive leadership style is necessary in order to get things done. This presents a dilemma for expatriates on aid projects. On the one hand they need to meet project objectives within the timescale set by the donor, on the other hand for a project to be truly developmental, it must allow for counterparts to learn to exercise good management practice on their own. This can be a slow and time-consuming process, which experience has shown is rarely achieved through project interventions.

Ideally, there should be a gradual move from an authoritarian leadership style to a participative and then a democratic style as counterparts gain in experience and confidence. Unfortunately the opposite can also happen. Most of the Sudanese projects revealed high levels of apathy among the counterparts which made the expatriates increasingly dis-illusioned about the latter's capacity to take over the running of the project. This encouraged them to assume both a more directive leader-ship style and an increasingly large share of the work so as to meet project targets, and to allocate mainly minor routine tasks to their coun-terparts. As a result they ended up both directing and implementing the project, which was totally counter-developmental. This in turn led to resentment on the counterparts' side at what they saw as the heavy-handed approach by the expatriates, and to increased apathy and non-cooperation. It was only when the counterparts were of relatively 'high maturity' at the start of the project that this negative trend did not occur (which helps to explain why aid projects are most successful in the more developed countries of the Third World — where in fact they are least needed).

The evidence showed that projects which are aimed at building up local capacity require a supportive and facilitating leadership style which is based on collaborative personal relationships and is learner and process oriented. At the same time, if the institution is characterized by low levels of expertise (not always as low as the expatriates presume), and a lack of discipline and accountability, a strong degree of direction and a well-structured work environment is required. The two are not easily compatible. The task-oriented, high pressure culture of the project combined with the expatriates' own desire for job satisfaction and a high standard of performance make it difficult for them to avoid an authoritarian leadership style.

Motivation

Motivation has come to be viewed by organizational psychologists as a significant factor in enhancing work performance (Maslow, 1954; Herzberg *et al*, 1959; Schein, 1980). And indeed motivation emerged from the Sudanese study as influencing the nature of project perform-ance significantly. High expatriate motivation set against low national motivation was yet one more example of an imbalance between the project and the host institution. This imbalance had a negative impact on the development aims of the project in that, as already stated, the expatriates were obliged to compensate for their counterparts' lack of motivation and resultant low input by taking on additional responsibil-ities in an effort to meet short-term goals.

Hersey and Blanchard (1982) consider motivating as one of the prime management functions, 'if motivation is low, employees' performance will suffer as much as if ability were low' (p. 4). Yet the need for motivation among local staff has rarely been given high priority in the context of aid projects, either in the theoretical literature or in agency design or evaluation models. One notable exception is Heaver (1982).

Herzberg *et al*'s two-factor theory of job-related needs (1959) offers an explanation for the different types and levels of motivation shown by the two parties on these projects. According to this model, local personnel would be seen as more concerned with environmental or 'hygiene' factors such as working conditions, interpersonal relations, money, status and security, because these represent unsatisfied needs. On the other hand the expatriates are more likely to be reasonably satisfied in this respect and to be more concerned with aspects of the job itself, the 'motivators', such as achievement, recognition of accomplishment, challenging work, increased responsibility and growth and development (Hersey and Blanchard, 1982, p. 58). It may be too simplistic to try and classify expatriates and Sudanese (or other groups of nationals) in this respect, and indeed there was evidence on these projects that some local personnel, albeit a minority, appeared highly motivated by self-actualization needs, while some expatriates were excessively concerned with job security and salary levels. Nevertheless, it did appear that individuals were motivated in different ways, and that tensions arose on the projects over their differing preoccupations. On the one hand, many Sudanese showed little incentive to work beyond a certain level in their official job with its low salary, poor promotion prospects and lack of professional support, and were often obliged to take on other work to supplement their meagre income. On the other hand, the expatriates had considerable interest in meeting the project objectives within the specified time limit (not least because their professional reputation and future career prospects were at stake) and were impatient at their counterparts' supposedly poor performance.

Herzberg's model is useful as an illustration of how tensions can arise on projects over different need priorities. It is true that the absence of realistic salary levels must be seen as a major barrier (but by no means the only one) to high levels of local participation on projects. If more realistic salaries were achieved, this would remove the principal concern with meeting basic living requirements, and, when linked to performance targets, would allow other higher-order needs to gain in importance (although it would also unfortunately serve to further isolate civil servants from the rest of the population in terms of income and lifestyle).

However, need satisfaction is not the only source of motivation in organizations. It can also be increased by a judicious choice of management style (as described above) and by greater participation in decision-making. In the face of very limited opportunities for public sector salary increases in the poorer countries of the world, Heaver (1982) makes suggestions for ways motivation can be improved by non-material incentive systems built on professional support and prestige, increased participation in decision-making and recognition of individual effort and achievement.

The Psychological Contract

Another source of low motivation on the Sudanese side and of further tension between expatriates and nationals lay in the weak psychological contract which prevailed in the host institution. According to Handy (1985) a psychological contract is an unwritten set of expectations operating between the employer and the employee as to what the organization on the one hand should provide to the employee and what he/she should give in return. For the employee, these expectations relate to such issues as pay, working hours, duties and promotion, while for the employer they concern loyalty, commitment and effort. Inherent in this concept is the employee's acceptance of the authority of his superiors, without which the organization cannot function. Where the organization fails to meet its employees' expectations, in particular with respect to pay and conditions, it loses some of its authority and employees may lower their performance levels. There is then a loss of faith and credibility on both sides; in fact the psychological contract has broken down. This is what had happened in Sudanese public sector institutions, and it affected project performance.

Handy identifies three types of psychological contract: coercive, calculative and cooperative, each of which works most effectively with a particular power source. A capacity-building development project would normally require a cooperative contract, because this is the only type that is entered into freely by both sides and which relies primarily on expert and personal power (a close relationship) and where new ideas and values are internalized and new attitudes and behaviour developed. However, such a contract would be difficult to arrive at in the circumstances described and indeed there were few signs of internalization of the change process on the projects studied.

In fact, in the host institutions studied the psychological contract was largely dysfunctional as local management's power source was weak and ineffectual, for the reasons already given, and employee motivation and performance levels were low. As senior officials also had little freedom to dismiss, discipline or withhold pay from a public sector employee, they were rarely able to enforce their authority, even through coercion.

At the same time, those in local management positions were themselves government employees and as such had their own expectations as to what the contract on their side should contain. In the Sudanese institutions they were as disillusioned as their staff in this respect and hence had little will to enforce the employer's side of the contract. In such a situation an implicit compromise contract is negotiated between managers and their staff which reflects the low level of reward available at all grades; the manager accepts low performance levels from the employee because he/she is performing in like manner, and he/she tacitly agrees not to impose sanctions or demand strict accountability. This is an inverted calculative contract: a mutually recognized low level of reward is met by mutually accepted levels of underachievement. This can be seen in many public sector institutions throughout the world.

In contrast, the psychological contract which prevailed between the expatriates and their employer (the donor) generated relatively high levels of motivation. This was a much stronger and more positive contract of a calculative/cooperative type based on resource and position power. Significantly, the expatriates expected the same level of commitment to the project by local managers and staff as they themselves were ready to give, despite the very different financial conditions which applied to the two sides.

Differing perceptions of the psychological contract made it difficult firstly for the expatriates to accept the justification for reduced levels of performance and accountability (concessions were only made very reluctantly after initial attempts to impose minimum standards had failed), and secondly for local personnel to understand that the project required increased commitment and effort (usually for little or no reward of any significance). The latter saw no logical basis for accepting such a contract, and, despite being seconded to the project, insisted on keeping to their existing type of contract (with its set of reduced expectations), which was incompatible with the demands of the project when translated into performance levels, targets and time schedules. This encouraged the expatriates to assume an authoritarian and directive leadership style, and at the same time to take on the major share of the workload.

In many Third World public institutions, a new dimension to the psychological contract has evolved. As we have seen, position and resource power on the side of the host institution were often replaced at senior levels by personal power. One feature of the exercise of this type of power is that individuals may owe their government positions to personal contacts rather than to any relevant aptitude or experience on their own part, in return for which they are expected to show loyalty to an individual rather than to the organization; this may be put to purposes which can be both legitimate (cooperation and effort in meeting organization goals) and illegitimate (carrying out personal instructions of an unofficial nature, even collusion in corrupt activities and cover-up). Subordinates may also be deterred from speaking too openly or too critically, or from acting in a non-conformist manner, for fear of jeopardizing their position. Such a psychological contract between two individuals rather than between the individual and the organization is usually dysfunctional and leads to official goals being displaced by personal or informal ones.

We can see, therefore, different psychological contracts prevailed on the expatriate and the local side. The weak contract on the Sudanese side acted as a brake on project performance and limited the options available to project managers in their pursuit of project aims.

What of the Education Project Beyond the Year 2000?

The analysis offered above, and the conclusions drawn from it, are based on a study of a small number of projects in one particular African country. However, it is likely that a similar scenario is being repeated many times over on institution-building projects, whether in education or in other sectors, in many developing countries. This will be especially the case in countries with weak infrastructure and low levels of expertise. This scenario would appear to be one of a marriage (between the project and the host institution) which has largely failed. As is most commonly the case in real life marriages, a major cause of failure would appear to be incompatibility — incompatibility between two personalities, or, in this case, between two organizational cultures. This incompatibility means that the two organizations are unable to work towards common goals; instead, each is pursuing its own agenda and its own set of goals, which are mutually irreconcilable. As a result, the chances of the project serving its original purpose of helping the local institution to plan and manage innovation in an atmosphere of cooperation and mutual trust is unlikely. Indeed the relationship which develops between the two, part confrontation part indifference[2], transforms the project from a supposedly developmental force into a counter-developmental force, because it tends to decrease rather than increase local capacity and makes the host institution more rather than less dependent on the donor for financial and human resources.

We need to remember that the development project has *always* been intended as a means of promoting locally sustainable initiatives, but that this goal has often been overshadowed by the fixation on the donor side with meeting project objectives within the prescribed budget and time allocations. The tendency has been to emphasize product rather than process, with the result that the institution-building and counterpart training functions of the project have all too often been downgraded.

So what then is the future of the education project if it is to retain any credibility as a vehicle of development and to fit within a donor strategy of supporting policy reform and local capacity-building? King (1992) gives donors an uncomfortable foretaste of what changes must come about if their new strategy is to be taken seriously. As he rightly points out, capacity building requires capacity utilization, not just by host governments but also by donors. Thus, he asks

> . . . does it build capacity or sustainability if all the project sup-
> plies are ordered through a combination of embassy privileges,
> the specialist departments of the agency, and the use of project
> expatriates? Does it build analytic capacity in the ministry if for
> every major aid project a separate project implementation unit
> is set up that effectively by-passes regular ministry channels? If
> over 90 per cent of the scholarship budget is allocated to train-
> ing in the donor country, and only a handful of fellowships are
> for *sur place* or third country training, it is unlikely that local
> institutional capacity is being built up systematically. If a project
> needs evaluating, does it support the local research centres at
> the university always to arrange for foreign consultants acting in
> their private capacity, rather than channelling funds through the
> institution? (p. 259)

And he sharply reminds donors that 'if the new rhetoric of local capacity-building is really carried through, donors will not be able to continue with business as usual. With the majority (. . .), they have scarcely begun to do the kind of policy analysis on their own aid programmes which they have been recommending to the recipients' (*ibid*, p. 262).

However, there is more to it than this. My analysis of what can go on inside a project in terms of the exercise of power and leadership, motivation and the prevailing psychology contract indicates that the organizational culture of the project as it is currently conceived and executed by the donor is fundamentally different to that prevailing in the host institution. This would suggest that, for the project to become more successful than it has been in assisting the development process, either the project or the host institution must change its organizational culture, so that the two are more mutually compatible.

The most obvious suggestion is for the host institution to become more like the project in its organizational culture. Indeed, the implicit assumption behind the institution-building project is that it is offering an organizational model for the host institution to emulate, i.e., one based on Western ideas of rationality and efficiency and Western models of good managerial practice. However, for the host institution to adopt the project's organizational culture would require not only structural and procedural change (in particular a reorientation of goals and a reduction in excessive bureaucratic procedures), but also a radical shift in values, attitudes and behaviour among local personnel and much higher levels of performance. This will not be easy to achieve for a number of reasons.

As already indicated, Third World bureaucracies have developed out of a particular political and sociocultural environment, and because of the lack of fit between official and unofficial/personal goals, individuals employed by them have tended to give priority to the latter. This means that, rather than operate in the service of the general public employees' efforts tend to be directed at meeting first and foremost their own social and economic needs. For the organization to ask them to redirect their efforts towards meeting official goals while still failing to meet their basic needs in terms of remuneration and job satisfaction is unrealistic. Even more seriously, the belief that local institutions lack managerial expertise and therefore all that is needed is for local managers to work alongside expatriate managers on a daily basis to acquire the relevant expertise, may well be misguided. According to Reilly (1987), contrary to popular belief Third World officials are already highly skilled and intelligent executives who manage the system with great efficiency to meet their own interests. For, what may appear to be structural weaknesses and irrational behaviour to the outsider are in fact structural strengths and quite rational behaviour from the inside, where the exercise of personal power, confusion, vagueness, low levels of accountability and reduced performance targets are advantages to the individual with a personal agenda. To change all this would be to upset the status quo and there is no incentive at the present time for those inside the system to do this. Furthermore, Moris (1977) refutes the implicit assumption of most Western management theories that management skills are transferable from one cultural setting to another. The administrative (organizational) culture is capable of neutralizing attempts at skills transfer, if this is perceived as a threat.

This then casts doubt on the advisability of the second option, that of bringing the project culture closer to that of the host institution, by integrating the project more fully into the latter's structures and procedures (part of which would involve an exclusive reliance on local channels for getting things done). While this might appear initially as a more development-friendly strategy, giving local personnel greater control over running the project and stimulating local capacity in particular in management, in fact it could be counter developmental for the reasons already given: Third World bureaucrats are working to a different (informal) agenda, one not usually directed at developmental goals. There may well be scope for increased efforts on the part of the donors to understand the organizational culture of the host institution within which they are working (and some donors are perhaps already attempting to do this), but any significant move at integrating the project and the host institution within an adverse bureaucratic culture is unlikely to produce the outcomes desired by donors.

Moreover, it is unlikely that shifting project practice through local channels will be acceptable to donor governments. This would slow down the implementation process to levels unacceptable to donors who have hawk-eyed Treasury officials looking over their shoulder. It would also have far-reaching implications for the employment of long-term expatriates on aid projects. There would be no place for zealous expatriates working to a set of precise short-term objectives set by the donor. At the most there could be built into the project some short-term visits to check on progress and offer advice and on-the-job training.

What this means in practice is that the policy reforms in education, as in other sectors, which the donors are insisting should be undertaken by would-be recipients of aid, will have to impinge not only on educational structures and processes (for example, introducing school fees, cutting funding to higher education, initiating more flexible training schemes for teachers) but also on the bureaucracy itself. This is already implicit in some donor demands, for example for a reduction in numbers of non-teaching staff and bureaucratic procedures in the education sector, and decentralization of educational administration, but they will have to go much further than that. Reform will have to involve a major shift in the value-system of the over-arching bureaucracy. The only way this can happen is if policy reform is seen to be in the interest of those who work within this bureaucracy. This cannot be brought about until formal and informal (personal) goals are brought close together and individuals see clearly the benefits to be derived from working towards official development goals (Heaver, 1982). This will be very difficult to do because the bureaucracy is embedded in a set of norms, values and behaviour patterns which are wedded to those prevailing in the wider society. Reform will therefore have to cut into the very fabric of society.

In the event, the cynic's view of the future is one of the donors continuing with 'business as usual' behind a facade of locally-initiated policy reform (which will uncannily resemble the latest donor pronouncements on what constitutes desirable policy) and of local capacity-building supported behind the scenes, discreetly or not so discreetly, by expatriates. The marriage will have failed, but to keep up appearances no divorce will be pronounced. Both partners will continue to follow their own agenda within an uneasy cohabitation.

Notes

1 Two decades ago, the American anthropologist GM Foster wrote of donor agencies 'today the greatest problem in technical assistance no longer is the client group but the innovating bureaucracy itself . . . a well established bureaucracy is more resistant to change than is the traditional agricultural village' (p. 11).
2 It is necessary to distinguish between personal/social relations between expatriates and nationals (which are often good) and professional relations (which are often poor). I am referring here to the latter.

References

COLCLOUGH, C. with LEWIN, K.M. (1993) *Educating All The Children: Strategies for Primary Schooling in the South*, Oxford, Clarendon Press.
FIEDLER, F. (1967) *A Theory of Leadership Effectiveness*, New York, McGraw Hill.
FOSTER, G.M. (1972) *Traditional Cultures and the Impact of Technological Change*, 2nd edition, New York, Harper and Brothers.
FRANKS, T. (1989) 'Bureaucracy, organisation culture and development', *Public Administration and Development*, 9, pp. 357–68.
HANDY, C. (1985) *Understanding Organisations*, 3rd edition, Harmondsworth, Penguin.
HANDY, C. and AITKEN, R. (1986) *Understanding Schools as Organizations*, London, Penguin.

HEAVER, R. (1982) *Bureaucratic Politics and Incentives in the Management of Rural Development*, World Bank Staff Working Paper 537, Washington, DC, World Bank.

HERSEY, P. and BLANCHARD, K.H. (1982) *Management of Organisational Behaviour: Utilizing Human Resources*, 4th edition, Englewood Cliffs, NJ, Prentice Hall.

HERZBERG, F., MAUSNER, B. and SNYDERMAN, B. (1959) *The Motivation to Work*, New York, John Wiley and Sons.

HOFSTEDE, G. (1980) *Culture's Consequences: International Differences in Work-Related Values*, Beverley Hills, CA, Sage.

HYDEN, G. (1983) *No Short Cuts to Progress*, London, Heinemann.

KING, K. (1992) 'The external agenda of aid in educational reform', *International Journal of Educational Development*, 12, 4, pp. 257–63.

MASLOW, A.H. (1954) *Motivation and Personality*, New York, Harper and Row.

MORIS, J. (1977) 'The transferability of Western management concepts and programs, an East African perspective', in BLACK, J.E., COLEMAN, J.S. and STIFEL, L.D. (Eds) *Education and Training for Public Sector Management in Developing Countries*, New York, Rockefeller Foundation.

REILLY, W. (1987) 'Management and training for development: The Hombe thesis', *Public Administration and Development*, 7, pp. 250–2.

ROETHLISBERGER, F.J. and DICKSON, W.J. (1939) *Management and the Worker*, Cambridge, MA, Harvard University Press.

SCHEIN, E.H. (1980) *Organisational Psychology*, 3rd edition, Englewood Cliffs, NJ, New Prentice Hall.

STUTLEY, P.W. (1980) 'Some aspects of the contemporary scene', in STONE, J.C. (Ed) *Experts in Africa*, Aberdeen, University of Aberdeen African Studies Group.

VERSPOOR, A. (1993) 'More than business-as-usual: Reflections on the new modalities of education aid', *International Journal of Educational Development*, 13, 2, pp. 103–12.

VROOM, V.H. and YETTON, P. (1973) *Leadership and Decision-Making*, Pittsburgh, PA, University of Pittsburgh Press.

Notes on Contributors

Beatrice Avalos-Bevan left Papua New Guinea, where she had spent six years as Professor of Education at the University of Papua New Guinea, in 1994, and is now working in the Ministry of Education in Santiago, Chile.

Lynn Davies is Director of the International Unit of the School of Education, University of Birmingham. She also heads the Faculty Division of the Graduate School, co-ordinating the provision and training for research students. She has lived and worked in Mauritius and Malaysia and researched education in various parts of Africa and Asia. Particular academic interests are in school management in developing countries; gender and management; and democratic school organisation. She has recently completed a book on *Study Skills for Teacher Training*.

Fiona Leach is a Lecturer in Education and Development at the Institute of Education at the University of London; prior to joining the Institute she worked extensively in Africa on British aid projects in education. Her current professional and academic interests are international aid to education, including alternatives to official donor assistance; project management and implementation; the cross-cultural transfer of knowledge and skills; gender, education and development, women and the labour market.

Thandike Mkandawire is Executive Secretary of CODESRIA, which is situated in Dakar, Senegal.

Geoffrey Partington, a Mancunian, is a graduate of Bristol, London, and Adelaide. He was a history teacher, headmaster, college lecturer and education officer before emigrating to Australia in 1976. He recently retired from the Flinders University of South Australia, but is currently teaching in the University of the South Pacific in Fiji.

Richard Pring was appointed Professor of Educational Studies and Director of the Department of Education at the University of Oxford in

1989, after twelve years as Professor of Education and Dean of the Faculty of Education at the University of Exeter.

Joseph Stetar is an Associate Professor and Director of the doctoral programme in higher education administration at Seton Hall University in South Orange, New Jersey, USA.

John D. Turner is Emeritus Professor of Education at the University of Manchester and a former Pro-Vice-Chancellor, and also President of the College of Preceptors. He has long experience in Africa where, after serving in Nigeria, Lesotho and Botswana, he was the first Vice-Chancellor at the University of Botswana.

Index